Law and
Legal Science

Law and Legal Science

An Inquiry into the Concepts
Legal Rule and *Legal System*

J. W. HARRIS

CLARENDON PRESS · OXFORD
1979

Oxford University Press, Walton Street, Oxford OX2 6DP

OXFORD LONDON GLASGOW
NEW YORK TORONTO MELBOURNE WELLINGTON
IBADAN NAIROBI DAR ES SALAAM LUSAKA CAPE TOWN
KUALA LUMPUR SINGAPORE JAKARTA HONG KONG TOKYO
DELHI BOMBAY CALCUTTA MADRAS KARACHI

© *J. W. Harris 1979*

British Library Cataloguing in Publication Data
Harris, James William
  Law and legal science.
  1. Legal rules   2. Law
  I. Title
  340.1′1   K237   78-41121

ISBN 0-19-825353-2

*Set by Gloucester Typesetting Co Ltd
and printed in Great Britain by
Richard Clay & Co Ltd, Bungay, Suffolk*

To
Jose

Contents

Abbreviations

C.A.L.	O. Hood Phillips: *Constitutional and Administrative Law*, 5th edn., 1973.
C.L.	H. L. A. Hart: *The Concept of Law*, 1961.
C.L.S.	J. Raz: *The Concept of a Legal System: an Introduction to the Theory of Legal System*, 1970.
C.U.	D. H. Hodgson: *Consequences of Utilitarianism: a Study in Normative Ethics and Legal Theory*, 1967.
D.N.	A. Ross: *Directives and Norms*, 1968.
E.H.K.	*California Law Review: Essays in Honor of Hans Kelsen*, 1971.
E.L.M.P.	H. Kelsen: *Essays in Legal and Moral Philosophy*, 1973.
E.L.P.	R. Summers (ed.): *Essays in Legal Philosophy*, 1968.
G.T.	H. Kelsen: *General Theory of Law and State*, 1945.
I.P.M.	J. Bentham: *An Introduction to the Principles of Morals and Legislation* (J. H. Burns & H. L. A. Hart, eds.), 1970.
J.D.	R. A. S. Wasserstrom: *Judicial Decision: Towards a Theory of Legal Justification*, 1961.
L.C.	G. Gottlieb: *The Logic of Choice: an Investigation of the Concepts of Rule and Rationality*, 1968.
L.F. (i)	K. Olivercrona: *Law as Fact*, 1939.
L.F. (ii)	K. Olivercrona: *Law as Fact*, 2nd edn., 1971.
L.M.S.	P. M. S. Hacker and J. Raz (eds.): *Law, Morality, and Society: Essays in Honour of H. L. A. Hart*, 1977.
L.V.	S. Munzer: *Legal Validity*, 1972.
N.A.	G. H. Von Wright: *Norm and Action*, 1963.
O.E.J.	A. W. B. Simpson (ed.): *Oxford Essays in Jurisprudence*, 2nd Series, 1973.
O.L.G.	J. Bentham: *Of Laws in General* (H. L. A. Hart, ed.), 1970.
O.L.J.	A. Ross: *On Law and Justice*, 1958.
P.E.L.	R. Cross: *Precedent in English Law*, 2nd edn., 1968.
P.J.D.	J. Austin: *The Province of Jurisprudence Determined, and the Uses of the Study of Jurisprudence*, 1954.
P.T.L.	H. Kelsen: *Pure Theory of Law*, 1967.

S.L.R.   H. Kelsen: 'Professor Stone and the Pure Theory of Law' (1965) 17 Stanford Law Review 1128.

T.R.S.   R. M. Dworkin: *Taking Rights Seriously* (revised impression) 1978.

W.J.   H. Kelsen: *What is Justice? Justice, Law, and Politics in the Mirror of Science*, 1957.

I

Introduction

1. THE CULTURAL SIGNIFICANCE OF THE CONCEPT LEGAL RULE

IN ANY developed society, discourse about the functioning of the legal process includes reference to 'rules'. This is true of discourse at every level of generality—from the friend who advises a motorist where it is 'safe' to park, to the essayist in comparative national constitutions. Talk about the police, the legal profession, the courts, or the constitution would be unimaginably different from what actually occurs if, *per impossibile*, the concept *legal rule* were banished from the societies in which it is now an implanted cultural datum.

This cardinal fact about legal discourse is not denied—though it is sometimes bemoaned—by those theorists who, in their analyses of legal processes, seek to play down the concept. They deny or qualify one or other, or both, of two assumptions which go hand in hand with everyday discourse about the law: first, that legal rules control decisions on the part of officials; second, that they ought to control them.

The first of these assumptions underlies two major legal enterprises; namely legislation and legal science. The commonest immediate objective of enacting statutes and legal regulations is to change patterns of decisions by judges and other officials, the ultimate objective being the advancement of some policy goal. This commonest immediate objective would be senseless if it were the case that official decisions are in no way controlled by legal rules. If judges and other officials always, or even generally, make the decisions they do as a result of a complex of motives which do not include accurate appraisal by them of the meaning-content of legislative materials, statute-making would be an inexplicably persistent social farce.

Legal science is that activity, widespread in countries with developed legal institutions, whose necessary objective is the systematic exposition of some corpus of legislative materials. A piece of legal science, to be such, must seek to describe what the law is on a topic by reference to relevant authoritative legislation. It may also offer historical explanations for the state of the law, or doctrine-based or policy-based criticisms of it, and recommendations for interpretation where the law is uncertain or for legislative amendment where it is unsatisfactory. Legal science is to be found in textbooks and treatises, in solicitors' advice and counsels' opinions and, commonly, in the reported decisions of courts.

If the decisions of officials were in no way controlled by legal rules appearing in legislative materials, legal science would be a pointless enterprise. Its basic data would not have the social relevance which its authors suppose them to have. It would also be a deleterious enterprise, since all those who rely on its products as guides to official decisions affecting them, would be wasting time, effort, and resources. Authors and consumers alike would be the victims of a 'high-class racket', a gigantic conceptual 'hoax',[1] the hoax that legal rules do actually govern, at least in the sense that official decisions would not be the same if they did not exist.

The second assumption which goes hand in hand with legal discourse—namely, that legal rules *ought* to control decisions by officials—is the foundation of the specific value of *legality*. When it is clear to all who know the contents of a rule and are acquainted with the facts, that the rule requires an official to make a particular decision, then it is contrary to legality if the official fails to make that decision.

The value of legality is a constituent element of the roles of all officials in societies with developed legal institutions. In this respect it is to be contrasted with the values attached to more specialized roles, such as those of judicial and legislative craftsmanship. It only applies to a situation in which an official

---

[1] Cf. F. Rodell: *Woe Unto you Lawyers*, 1959.

knows of a rule and its application is beyond doubt. Breach of legality must therefore be a conscious act.

So much is observance of legality an accepted part of the role of officials, that an announced departure from it rarely occurs, at least in the day-to-day domestic administration of a state. An official would not be performing his office if he were heard to say: 'I have no doubt that this legal rule which is binding on me requires me to do X, but I intend to do Y.' Such an announced breach with legality, if made by an important official, would be seen as precipitating a constitutional crisis.

A breach with legality will therefore normally involve either concealment or sham. Secret breaches of legality may occur in any society. An open breach with legality, in which an official pretends that rules have an effect which everybody knows they do not, is likely to occur often only in a terroristic society whose rulers think it worth while to make a pretence of legality—for instance, by staging sham trials.

The assumption that legal rules ought to control official decisions is the foundation of the value of legality. It is this fundamental aspect of it which is generally immune from announced violation. The value of legality is also commonly invoked in connection with the procedure by which officials ascertain whether a rule applies to a particular case. It is said to be contrary to legality, for instance, if a disputant before a tribunal is not given an opportunity to advance evidence.

These assumptions about the relation of legal rules to official decisions are of different logical types: the one empirical and causal, and the other evaluative and justificative. Yet the value of legality would be empty if either were ill-founded. So also would be the closely associated value of constitutionality, which, among other things, requires officials to choose among conflicting rules according to certain criteria, and which requires legislatures, in laying down rules, to observe certain procedures. These aspects of the value of constitutionality would be robbed of their present significance if it were not assumed both that legal rules ought to, and that they do, control decisions on the part of officials.

If these assumptions were not well-founded, the practices of legislation and legal science, and the values of legality and constitutionality, would dissolve into pointless charades. Against this fact there must be set the following stark truth: in any particular case in which an official has made a decision, it cannot be *proved* (logically, or as a matter of fact) that he could not consistently, or would not, have made that decision if legislative source-materials binding on him had not contained a particular rule. The application of pre-existing rules to subsequently arising facts always, in theory, involves purposive elements, so that the official is always, logically, free to make more than one decision, and in consequence the decision he does make does not express a proposition which is logically entailed by the rule. The actual motives operating on an official—if 'motive' is taken to include subconscious predilections of all kinds—are unwitnessable both by others and by the official himself, so that it can never be shown as a matter of fact that the rule *caused* his act of deciding.

It is a commonplace that the application of rules is often unclear and that officials may have conscious or unconscious biases which lead them into particular interpretations. The point here is that it can never be shown that an official came to the decision he did solely because of a rule.

That this is so as a matter of strict logic can be illustrated with an extreme, hypothetical example. A statute provides: 'No child under the age of ten years may be convicted of any criminal offence.' A child is arraigned on a charge of theft. During the trial, undisputed evidence is adduced to prove beyond any doubt that (a) the child committed all the elements of the offence, but that (b) he is only seven years old. The judge discharges the child.

The statute says: 'No child . . .' But supposing the point had been taken that the statute had made no mention of race, so that it was open to the court to interpret the legislative intention to have been to exclude from conviction only children of a favoured race and not those of the race to which the defendant belonged. If the court had taken this point and had convicted the child, legality would manifestly have been breached, because the judge would have found that the rule did not apply to the case when it was clear to all that it did. Such a decision would be possible only in a society in which sham legality was practised.

And yet the decision to exclude such an interpretation is not strictly logical, but purposive, in nature. Words like 'no', 'any', or 'all', when appearing in legislative materials, do not have the function of categorical symbols in a deontic logic, because one can never rule out the possibility that reasons could be found for interpreting them as being subject to exceptions. (Consequently, symbolic logics have little practical relevance to legal interpretation; and computerization of legislative source materials is unlikely ever to be of assistance in the application, as opposed to the storage, of the law.)

The reason why, in the example given, no interpretation of the statute which limited its scope to children of the more favoured race could be given, without contravening legality, is that it would be clear to everyone that that was not the purpose of the rule. That its purpose was to remove *all* young children from the ambit of the criminal law could not be genuinely disputed.

This would be true even in present-day societies which practice legal discrimination against racial or other groups. Even in these, distinctions are likely to be expressed in legislation rather than implied by way of interpretation. And where sham legality is alleged to take place in such societies, the accusation usually is, not that unsupportable purposive interpretations were given to rules, but that rules were only made applicable by findings of fact which plainly contradicted the evidence. In our example, this sort of sham legality would occur if, despite voluminous evidence that the child was born only seven years ago, the judge ruled that he was aged ten.

One could of course imagine a society in which the persecution of a particular racial group was such an announced and accepted social goal that the suggested interpretation of the statute would not contravene legality. It would have to be a society in which some such plea as the following could genuinely —that is, without indulging in sham legality—be urged: 'It would be absurd to suppose that the legislature intended that children of the (less favoured) race should be exempted, because their peculiar aptness to form criminal intent is notorious, and therefore the court ought to interpret the statute by reading "No child" to mean "No child of the (more favoured) race".' Universal agreement about the purpose of a particular kind of legal rule excludes the possibility of such an argument being upheld, without contravention of legality, in any present-day society.

If the contingent fact of unanimity in the rejection of certain purposive interpretations of rules is recognized, then deontic logic becomes a legitimate species of deductive logic, and it follows deductively that a child below the minimum age cannot be prosecuted. If two people agree that if a tossed coin comes down heads, X has first innings in a game of cricket, and the coin comes down heads, no one would describe an assertion by Y—'Ah yes, but the rule was only applicable when the sun was shining'—as anything else than a cheat. (It would be otherwise if the parties lived in a society where it was accepted by some that chance only operated properly in the sunshine.) Similarly, a purposive application of the minimum-age rule so as to exclude its application from children of the less favoured race would universally be regarded as contrary to legality.

It might be objected that literal 'unanimity' in rejection of certain purposive interpretations can never be relied upon. Might there not always be at least one crank found to argue, for example, that, in view of the extraordinary criminal propensities of infant redheads, it cannot have been part of the legislative purpose to exclude them? If this objection were valid, it would apply to every attempt to explain the intellectual processes of any social-scientific discipline. The criteria of relevance of points taken within a social-scientific debate must have an outer limit fixed by general assumptions about human institutions, even though the limit varies with time and place. 'Unanimity' refers to the opinions of those whom one can expect to be accepted as serious participants in such a debate.

It is necessary to distinguish two quite different roles which 'purpose' plays in the law. Where the application of the law is clear, where only one decision can be given consistently with legality, unanimity about the purpose of particular kinds of rules operates negatively to exclude interpretations which would be contrary to legality. Here no evidence of the Legislature's, or anyone else's, individual purpose is required. In unclear cases, however, one class of reasons sometimes advanced for advocating an interpretation relates (as we shall see in chapter five) to the particular, proven 'purpose' of some person or persons involved in the legislative process. Here 'purpose' operates positively, and what the purpose was is often a matter of serious debate.

Thus, if the judge discharges the seven-year-old child, one cannot, strictly, assert that the logical force of the rule compelled him so to do and in that sense *prove* that the rule controlled his decision. Even with the rule, he might (as a matter of strict logic) have come to a different decision. Nevertheless, the decision can be described as a practical deduction if certain universal purposive assumptions are added to the rule as grounds of his decision.

The second sense in which it may be urged that one cannot prove that an official makes a particular decision because of the content of a particular rule relates to the possible operation of subconscious motives. The judge might have discharged the seven-year-old child even if the statutory rule had not existed, by employing legal or sham legal purposive interpretations of other rules. He might have been predisposed to do so because of all kinds of predilections which urge him in that direction, of which neither he nor any observer is conscious.

If a judge discharges one child, giving the statutory rule as his reason, we cannot be sure that he would not have convicted another child, nor that he would not convict the first child on another occasion, because it might be that predilections operating on him on this occasion would not operate on other occasions. Such suggestions seem incredible but cannot be disproved simply because the circumstances of such a decision-making process cannot be exactly reproduced, so that no strictly authenticated verification is possible.

We are thus left with a seeming paradox. On the one hand, important legal practices and values presuppose, and every day legal discourse takes for granted, that legal rules do and ought to control decisions on the part of officials. On the other hand, that any particular such decision was controlled by a rule can never be proved by logic alone, nor by experimental test. The only arbiter is 'common sense', that is, assumptions based on generalizations from personal experience and not falsified by counter-instances.

But common sense is likely to vary in its judgments. In the example given above of the discharged child, it will adjudge that legal discourse, practices, and values are right to give unique importance to the operation of the rule and to discount theoretical bars to proof of its effective operation. If the legislature introduces a new rule changing the minimum age of criminal liability, with the immediate purpose of securing that officials will not convict children below that age, no one would express the least doubt that its objective would be attained through the effective application of the new rule. If anyone seeking information as to the content of the law reads in a textbook that there is a rule fixing a minimum age, no one could doubt that he had thereby acquired useful knowledge.

On the other hand, if the rule under consideration were one which made it a criminal offence to 'conspire to corrupt public morals', the fact that a conviction or acquittal cannot be proved to be controlled by the rule is significant. Conflicts between different purposive interpretations, any of which could be accepted without contravening legality, must arise. And when the *protasis* of the rule was adjudged to apply to a particular case, it would be, even from a commonsense standpoint, extremely difficult to assess whether or not subconscious predilections had operated.

The importance of the actual meaning-content of such a rule would accordingly be reduced. By enacting such a rule, a legislature could not hope to produce any predictable shift in patterns of official decisions, unless account were taken of known official views about purpose and known official biases. The legal scientist would convey minimal information if he merely set out the content of the rule. The charge of contravening legality would scarcely be possible in the case of any decision 'applying' the rule. It would be otherwise if we were informed that, as well as the general rule, there was, subsumed under it, a more specific rule making it an offence to publish a directory advertising the services of prostitutes.[1] The more specific rule could be applied in situations in which its applicability could not be sensibly controverted.

In the case of any particular legal rule, it would be extremely difficult to keep a tally of the number of occasions on which it clearly applied, and to compare this with the number of occasions on which its possible application raised questions of pur-

---

[1] Cf. the decision of the House of Lords in *Shaw* v. *Director of Public Prosecutions* (1962) A.C. 220, approved in *Knuller* (*Publishing, Printing and Promotions*) *Limited* v. *Director of Public Prosecutions* (1973) A.C. 435.

posive interpretation. No evidence whatever of the correlation can be expected to be reflected in the reports of litigated cases. The mistaken assumption that it can, lies at the root of many of the sceptical views about rules expressed by writers considered in the next chapter as representatives of the disputes theory of law.

Where disputes are settled by judges following arguments about the law, there is a good chance that different purposive interpretations of rules will be arguable without contravening legality. A disputes theory of law fastens on such occasions as typical of the application of rules. But outside the courts, before there is any dispute, legal rules apply deductively (given unanimity in purposive interpretation) to countless situations.

Where a notice by a roadside specifies a speed limit, streams of passing motorists know that to exceed it will constitute an offence, and decide whether or not to risk being caught. Every time that one of them registers what the law is and how it applies to him, law is applied deductively. After 999 such motorists have passed the sign, the thousandth comes by carrying a passenger to hospital. He may not know whether, if he speeds, he will be committing an offence. A lawyer sitting at his elbow who knows the relevant regulations may not be able to tell him either, because although the definition of the offence is baldly stated, a purposive interpretation which excludes such a case may be arguable. If there is a prosecution, there may then, perhaps, be a dispute.[1] The example of the discharged seven-year-old child is extremely unlikely to occur in practice precisely because everyone would assume that the rule would control the court's decision, and there would therefore be no point in the prosecution.

There are enough rules approximating to the minimum-age-liability type or to the speed-limit type, rather than to the conspiracy-to-corrupt type, to place the usefulness of rule-based

---

[1] The defence of necessity has a very limited scope in English law. The Court of Appeal has held that drivers of fire engines crossing red traffic lights would be technically guilty of an offence, however great the emergency, because nothing in the wording of the relevant legislation indicates an exception. Nevertheless, it was said that it would be proper for the police never to prosecute or if they did, for Justices always to grant an absolute discharge; and the Court held that an order from the chief officer of the fire brigade directing this 'unlawful' conduct to be undertaken was a lawful order—*Buckoke* v. *Greater London Council* (1971) Ch. 662. Cf. *Johnson* v. *Phillips* (1975) 3 All E.R. 682.

discourse, practices, and values beyond doubt. Legal regulations stipulating what must or may be done by reference to time, measure, number, or amount impinge on many areas of life, especially those enmeshed with large-scale organizations; and many legal rules, whose basis is not numerical, yet define the area to which they apply by reference to a standard which is precise enough to make it possible to identify many occasions as undoubtedly coming within its scope. Although in certain areas there is a tendency to substitute the discretion of courts or other officials for any attempt to pre-empt conclusions by rules, the over-all trend is probably the other way. In many societies, increasing material interdependence, coupled with decreasingly effective face-to-face social mechanisms, leads to greater reliance on detailed legal regulation by the state.

2. THE LOGIC OF LEGAL SCIENCE— 'RULE' AND 'SYSTEM'

I have argued that the application of law to clear cases is, in a broad sense, 'deductive'. Unless the word 'logic' is to be reserved for analytical reasoning approximating to a mathematical model, then any kind of argument in which a particular conclusion is supported by a general warrant is a logical argument.[1]

So far as the application of legal rules to particular instances is concerned, legal logic does not differ greatly from any kind of practical logic. But so far as relations between legal rules are concerned, legal science has its own special 'logic'.[2]

The rule-systematizing logic of legal science, as I shall try to demonstrate, is comprised of four principles—exclusion, subsumption, derogation, and non-contradiction.

By 'exclusion' is meant that principle in accordance with which legal science presupposes a determinate number of independent legislative sources for any legal system, and thereby identifies the system.

---

[1] Cf. S. E. Toulmin: *The Uses of Argument*, 1958.

[2] Toulmin takes 'jurisprudence' to be the best model for sound arguments—op. cit., pp. 7–10, 96. But whatever value his jurisprudential model has for the logic of arguments in general, it is of only limited value for jurisprudence itself. This is because Toulmin ignores rule-systematizing arguments.

By 'subsumption' is meant that principle in accordance with which legal science makes hierarchical connections between legal rules originating in superior and inferior legislative sources.

By 'derogation' is meant that principle in accordance with which legal science rejects a rule, or part of a rule, because of its conflict with another rule originating in a superior source.

By 'non-contradiction' is meant that principle in accordance with which legal science rejects the possibility of describing a legal system in such a way that one could affirm the existence of a duty, and also the non-existence of a duty, covering the same act-situation on the same occasion.

None of these principles deals with the way in which legal rules are applied to facts. They are none the less here termed 'logical' since they refer to standard reasoning-steps forming an integral part of a certain mental discipline, the practice of legal science.

These principles have a function analogous to the principles of classical logic. First, they are principles about the cognitive arrangement of semantic entities, albeit normative propositions rather than factual propositions. Second, they are generally observed, not because of the authority of anyone who has formulated them, nor because of their appeal to conscience or their support by sanctions or social pressure, but because the field of knowledge which they help to construct would soon lose its usefulness if they were generally disregarded.

Legal science deploys its own peculiar logic when it exercises its own defining function, that is, when it describes the law. In one of the senses in which the expression 'legal system' is used, the legal system of a community corresponds precisely with the *law now in force* in that community. In this sense of the expression—and as I shall argue in this sense only—a legal system is exclusively comprised of legal rules.

In this sense, the concept legal system, like the concept legal rule, is presupposed by the value of legality. Legality requires officials, not merely to apply legal rules, but also to apply only those legal rules which are identifiable as members of their system. What their system is depends on the independent legislative sources which, consistently with the value of constitutionality, they are required to recognize.

Officials (especially judges) are also required to apply rules systematically. It is not enough that a particular official decision can, without infringing legality, be described as the application of an individual legal rule, nor that the rule in question can, without infringing constitutionality, be described as originating in one of the permitted sources. It must also be shown—if the matter is at all disputed—that the decision is consistent with the system as a whole.

From this it follows that the decision-making official must himself act as a legal scientist. All the law on the topic to which the decision belongs must be known and, as has been said, it is the peculiar function of legal science to state the law on particular topics. Of course, the topic to which a decision relates may not be large. That is to say, there may not be many act-situations covered by the law of which the behaviour being considered by the official is an example. Consequently, acting as a legal scientist may not be a problem for the official. If it is, he may accept the legal-science conclusions about what the law is, reached by someone else whose opinion he can trust. Nevertheless, in principle he must act as a legal scientist, since it is not enough for him to apply *any* legal rule originating in a proper source. It is part of his office to apply the *right* rule, or combination of rules, reading the legal system ('the law') as a whole. This systematizing of rules is done by means of the four logical principles of legal science described above.

It will be one of the principal contentions of this book that the concepts *legal rule* and *legal system* are legitimately used to give shape to dissimilar elements constituting the subject matter of different kinds of social appraisal. For example, if we are discussing social action on the psychological level, it is legitimate to use the concept legal rule in the sense of what I shall describe as a 'rule-idea'. If, however, we are concerned to make a behavioural description of society, we may use the concept legal rule in the sense of a 'rule-situation'.

In one sense, as has been said, 'legal system' means a system of rules constituting the present law. In another sense it means a historic congeries of rules, principles, policies, doctrines, and maxims, forming part of an official tradition. Legal science, as we shall see, employs the concept in either of these senses, depending on whether it is exercising a descriptive or critical function. There is a third sense in which the expression is used by the social sciences generally, and in non-technical discourse, as a relatively vague way of referring to complex institutional structures. Such structures are to be found in all modern states, centring on courts and radiating out to other institutions, such as prisons, police forces, administrators and so on. The expression 'developed legal system' is commonly used to refer to the typical panoply of such institutions to be found in a contemporary industrialized society.

The next chapter discusses conceptions of legal rule and legal system expressed by or implicit within certain theoretical writings. The purpose will be, not to offer an exhaustive analysis of the contributions to jurisprudence of the theorists discussed, but to indicate that their different versions of these conceptions are serviceable (to varying degrees) for different types of general inquiry about the law. The bases laid for different types of inquiry will be classified as different 'theories of law', and the conception of legal rule and of legal system presented by each such theory will be described as a 'theorem'.

I shall not argue that any of these conceptions of rule or system is intrinsically right, nor shall I consider whether any of them approaches more nearly than the others to the every-day usage of any particular words. It is hoped, however, by the comparison between them, to throw light on social practices, values, and institutions which presuppose the concepts.

In particular we are concerned with the practices and values of legal science. It will be contended that, although the concepts *legal rule* and *legal system* mean different things in different kinds of inquiry, their use in combination is peculiarly appropriate to the sense in which they stand for normative meaning-contents (that is, *must, must not*, or *may* propositions). Thus, although one may legitimately speak of a 'legal rule' and mean a rule-idea or rule-situation, and of a 'legal system' and mean an institutional complex or a traditionary congeries of principles, if one speaks of rules as 'members' of systems, or of systems as 'being comprised' of rules, both concepts must (if one is speaking consistently) be purely normative. They must stand for units of meaning, abstracted from social behaviour-patterns and from psychological events. In the pure-norm sense, a legal system is a *field of normative meaning*, and a legal rule is part of such a field.

Much of interest may be said about society in terms of other conceptions of legal rule or legal system. In particular, contributions to political theory have often made use of the concept legal system (laws of a community) in some sense other than the pure-norm sense, the object being to stress some institutional feature of political societies, or to demarcate the role played by violence in a political society. Again, the sociology of law may employ the concept legal system in some institutional sense, or the concept legal rule in the sense of rule-idea or rule-situation.

It is here contended, however, that the pure-norm versions of these concepts are also essential to any adequate sociology of law and any comprehensive political theory. The officials who man the institutions of developed political societies must themselves at times act as legal scientists, or accept the advice of legal scientists. The institutionalized force, which is a universal feature of stable modern societies, takes the form it does because those who wield it presuppose (1) the values of legality and constitutionality, and hence (2) the discipline of legal science with its own special logic, and hence (3) the pure-norm conceptions of legal rule and legal system.

3. THE TASKS OF GENERAL JURISPRUDENCE

The tasks which general jurisprudence may set itself can be divided into four overlapping categories: first, inquiries into the relation of law and morality; second, the production of an improved vocabulary for the use of lawyers; third, inquiries into the logical status of statements in the science of law; fourth, socio-political inquiries about societies under law.

(A) *Law and morality*

'The relation of law to morality' may, as Professor Hart has said, cover several distinguishable kinds of question, of which he instances the following: first, to what extent has the historical development of law been influenced by morality, and vice versa? Second, must some reference to morality enter into an adequate definition of 'law' or 'legal system'? Third, to what sorts of moral criticisms is law appropriately subject? Fourth, is the fact that conduct is by certain standards immoral sufficient to justify its punishment by law?[1]

No attempt is made in this book to say anything about the answers to the first and fourth of these questions; although discussion about both may be clarified if we first decide whether by 'law' we mean the normative field of meaning which is the subject-matter of descriptive legal science, or one of the other conceptions of legal rule or legal system here distinguished.

In view of the focus of attention given here to law as the subject-matter of descriptive legal science, the second question has to be answered in the negative. 'Rules of law', to be described as such by legal science, do not as I shall argue in chapter four, have to pass any general standards of critical morality.

The third question is partly dealt with in chapter five, where we compare various criteria according to which the legal scientist or legal official may make decisions where legality gives no clear guide, and where we consider one recent attempt to subsume these criteria under a single coherent theory of judicial decision-making (Professor Dworkin's Rights Thesis). The models of rationality described in chapter five indicate certain kinds of reason which may be given to justify value-choices in the development of the law. It is a matter of terminology whether these criteria are referred to as 'moral'.

The discussion of models of rationality is at best only a partial answer to the third of Hart's law-morality questions. We do not discuss in this book whether there are any specially appropriate moral criteria by reference to which settled rules of law can be criticized. Nor do we discuss whether there are any general moral-political principles in accordance with which the role of legal scientist or legal official may be subsumed under 'the good life'. To do this, it would be necessary to consider, among other things, what sort of moral status (if any) the values of legality and constitutionality have, and to what extent they are rightly to be subordinated to other moral claims.[2] They are relative values only. It is part of the role of a legal scientist *qua* legal scientist, and of a legal official *qua* legal official, to apply rules

---

[1] *Law, Liberty and Morality*, 1963, pp. 1–4.
[2] Cf. A. M. Honoré: 'Social Justice', *E.L.P.*, p. 61, where 'the justice of conformity to rule' is compared with other requirements of social justice.

to be found in legislative source-materials to cases, and only such rules as originate in the *proper* sources. According to critical ethics, however, it may be that he ought not to act as a legal scientist or legal official. This may be so if, according to some critical criterion, the social institutions which produced the relevant legislative source-materials are morally unacceptable.

(B) *The improvement of legal vocabulary*

Legal practitioners have been unfavourably compared with medical men and engineers because of their lack of a consistent scientific vocabulary.[1] Terms like 'right', 'duty', 'property', 'person', and 'possession' are continually used by lawyers as terms of art, but nowhere are they used with consistency. If this slipshod terminology were replaced by greater precision, it would be easier to make precise descriptive statements about the law.

Analytic jurists, from Bentham onwards, have attempted to stipulate greater precision, but with little effect on the practice of legal science. Before the objective could be attained, agreement would have to be reached on two fundamental matters.

First, agreement would have to be reached as to the structure of the basic units described by legal science. If we disagree as to the logical parts, there is no point in trying to agree on their names.

The problem of structure is dealt with in chapter three. It may be noted here, however, that those who in twentieth-century Anglo-American jurisprudence have tried hardest to provide an improved legal vocabulary have taken 'jural relations' as basic. For the followers of W. N. Hohfeld, the fundamental legal conceptions are jural relations created by legal rules. If a legal rule has a bearing on an act or omission of X, and that act or omission if performed might affect Y, $Y/1 \ldots Y/n$, n. jural relations have been created. Persons born in the same jurisdiction will be from birth related, each to each, by the most general rules of the constitution. More specific relations will be created by statutory rules, factory regulations, particular rules emanating from contracts and law-suits, and so on down to the very close jural relation created by an unconditional order directing a hangman to execute a prisoner.

[1] J. H. Wigmore, in A. Kocourek: *Jural Relations*, 2nd edn., 1928, p. xii.

Hohfeld attempted to categorize types of legal relation by reference to levels of legal implementation;[1] but he recognized that such categorization is determined merely by convenience of exposition.[2]

Hohfeld does not deny the logical priority of the concept *legal rule* over *legal relation*. I shall argue that in all contexts descriptive information about the law may conveniently be given in terms of rules. The concept legal relation, on the other hand, is of use to legal science only when a litigious context requires legal information to be expressed about a pair of actual or potential opponents. Since the discipline of legal science is not exclusively court-centred, the logically prior unit is also the more convenient unit.

The second prerequisite of a precise vocabulary for legal science is the abandonment, as one of the possible models of rationality used in developing the law, of the model I shall call the 'doctrine model'. This would be a painful piece of surgery for legal science. Since its emergence as a distinct discipline, legal science has included, as well as descriptions of the rules valid at the time of writing, generalized statements about legal concepts and values which influence (or appear to influence) the decision of doubtful cases. Development of the law by reference to such (relatively) vague principles and policies constitutes application of the 'doctrine model' of rationality.

As already indicated, the concept legal system is sometimes used by legal science to refer to a historic congeries of such principles. In describing both 'the law' (in the sense of the present system of valid rules) and 'the law' (in the sense of the congeries of principles, policies, doctrines, and maxims traditionally employed by a community's officials in unclear cases), legal science commonly makes use of the *same* terminology. Terminological precision would only be possible if *different* terms were used to indicate the content of rules from those used to indicate the content of principles and policies. Legal technicians would have to make up their minds, for example, whether the word 'right' was to stand for a particular common feature of the

---

[1] W. N. Hohfeld: *Fundamental Legal Conceptions as Applied in Judicial Reasoning*, 1919, pp. 69, 108 ff. 'Relations Between Equity and Law' (1913), 11 Mich. L.R. 537, 551, 553, 567, n. 24, 567–8, n. 27.

[2] 'Relations Between Equity and Law' (1913), 11 Mich. L.R., p. 569, n 32.

structure of legal rules, or for an aspirational goal embodied in legal principles.

A general 'scientific vocabulary' could only be achieved if theoretical agreement were reached on questions of structure and if practical separation were achieved between the descriptive and critical functions of legal science. Neither eventuality is likely.

Nevertheless, particular (as opposed to general) jurisprudence rightly concerns itself with the actual usage of particular terms in legislative materials, especially in the context of judge-made law. This is justified precisely because 'chameleon-hued words' —to use Hohfeld's expression[1]—may be used without their ambiguities being appreciated, and consequently a considered legislative choice may be impeded. Such particular jurisprudence, of which Hohfeld's analysis of the judicial usage of terms like 'right' and 'privilege' is a good example, should apply itself, not to principles and values of universal scope, but to the development of particular areas of positive law.

Much critical legal literature employs this method on occasion. Whether one wishes to describe essays about positive law as 'jurisprudential'—in the sense of particular jurisprudence— or not, will be a matter of degree, depending on the emphasis laid on the part played by concepts and the word standing for them in the law's development. There is thus a continuum between particular jurisprudence and (non-jurisprudential) critical legal science.

(C) *The logical status of legal-scientific statements*

The third task of general jurisprudence consists of inquiries into the logical status of statements in legal science. For two hundred years legal positivists have assumed that the question 'what is law' is equivalent to the question 'what does the legal practitioner mean by "law"?' If statements in legal science are factual assertions, then 'law' is some sort of fact; but if they are evaluations, then 'law' is some sort of evaluative criterion. Accordingly, the logic of legal science is where jurisprudence should begin. In the words of Professor Alf Ross: 'The subject of jurisprudence is not law, nor any part or aspect of it, but the study

---

[1] Op. cit., p. 35.

of law. Jurisprudence dwells, so to speak, one storey higher than the study of law and "looks down" upon it.'[1]

Once theorists directed their attention to actual, as opposed to ideal, law, it was soon discovered that substantive rules common to all systems were not to be found. It was thought, however, that the clue to the logic of legal science resided in the fact that everywhere those who describe positive law employ a common battery of conceptual terms—'right', 'duty', 'person', 'property', and so forth—the 'principles, notions and distinctions' which John Austin said were common to the 'maturer systems'.[2]

This has turned out to be a false clue for many reasons. As stated earlier, lawyers use these terms with notorious imprecision. Furthermore, many of these terms are shared with morals, so that their analysis is unlikely to throw light on any differences there may be between the logic of moral discourse and that of legal science. And in any case, the community of concepts may be a historical accident, rather than logic-determined. It so happens that the 'maturer systems' derive their vocabulary either from Roman law or from English Common Law, so that, provided these historical systems used a particular term in approximately similar ways, we have a universal concept. Where they markedly diverged over use of terms—as with 'possession' or 'ownership'—the universal conceptual analyst is stumped.

To understand its logic, we must examine, not terms, but the intellectual discipline of legal science itself. When lawyers sieve legislative source-materials, in order to achieve topic-related conclusions of law, what conjunctions and disjunctions do they employ, upon what intellectual operations are they engaged?

Hans Kelsen believed that his 'Pure Theory of Law' provided answers to such questions:

[T]he pure theory of law has opened the way to the viewpoint from which the law may be understood as an 'ideology' in this specific sense:—as a system of connections different from that of nature. The possibility and necessity of such a discipline directed towards the law as a normative meaning is proved by the fact that the science of law has been in existence for millennia—a science which, as dog-

[1] *O.L.J.*, pp. 25-6.   [2] *P.J.D.*, p. 365.

matic jurisprudence, serves the intellectual needs of those who deal
with the law.[1]

The 'system of connections' which legal science imposes upon
raw legislative material is indeed different from those which
natural science imposes upon empirical phenomena. In other
words, the logic of legal science is different from the classic logic
of synthetic propositions. It exhibits the four principles of exclusion, subsumption, derogation, and non-contradiction—all of
which are recognized (expressly or implicitly) in Kelsen's
writings.[2]

It is one of the principle aims of this book to investigate the
primary descriptive activity of legal science. We shall accordingly be concerned to inquire into the logical status of statements made by legal scientists when they purport to describe
the present law on a topic, that is, when they convey information about part of the 'legal system' in the sense of a momentary
system of valid rules. However, the 'intellectual needs of those
who deal with the law' have no paramount claim, as Kelsen's
theory suggests they have. Their contribution to social life will
be set alongside that of other social inquiries about 'the law'.
This requires 'law', as the subject-matter of descriptive legal
science, to be contrasted with 'law', as the subject matter of
other social sciences, and entails the denial of any univocal
theory of 'law'.

The view that will be propounded is that statements in legal
science may describe any part of that normative field of meaning which stipulates the legal duties and exceptions to duty
existing at the time of writing. There are, however, good reasons
why this normative field of meaning should primarily be divided
into units called 'positive legal rules'. It is in terms of such units
that the values of legality and constitutionality are expressed,
and it is to such units that the four logical principles of legal
science apply.

The internal structural elements of each positive legal rule, it
will be argued, are three in number; the act-situation which is

[1] *P.T.L.*, p. 105.
[2] Although Kelsen denied that legal logic was a special logic (*E.L.M.P.*, p. 251),
his persistent rejection of methodological syncretism amounts to a recognition that
—as the word 'logic' is used in this chapter—legal science does have its own peculiar
logic.

the subject of the duty or exception from duty, an *ought* or *may* deontic operator, and the specification of the conditions under which the duty or exception from duty exists. A fourth structural element of a statement describing a positive legal rule is the specification of its source.

The values and logical procedures of legal science could be interpreted as applying to rules with a different structure, namely, to rules directed only towards officials, stipulating sanctions—the structure advocated by Kelsen and Ross. I shall argue that the structure outlined above is to be preferred on the ground that it provides a better basis for the critical functions of legal science and on the ground that it provides a more convenient basis for legal sociology.

The view here suggested of the basic units of which legal systems are comprised is reductionist in nature. It means that descriptive statements in legal science which are not descriptive of duty-imposing or duty-excepting rules are reducible to statements about the conditions under which the duties imposed by various rules exist. Such reductionism is a necessary consequence of the logic and values of legal science.

This reductionism applies, however, only to descriptive legal science. Legal-science statements may not be descriptive of the present law. They may be overtly critical of it; or they may be sociological in character—for instance, when they compare rules of law with observable, behaviourally-based, social rules ('rule-situations'). Further, they may present historical explanations for the law having reached its present state or predict its future development. Legal science also typically describes established policies, principles, and doctrines which have been used to guide (or justify) the decisions of certain classes of officials, which together comprise part of the tradition of a legal community and which constitute a non-momentary 'legal system'.

The description of the legal duties which exist at the time of writing is the primary, but not the only (and often not the most interesting), function of legal science. It is, however, crucial for an understanding of the intellectual processes of legal science that the descriptive function should be differentiated as clearly as possible from these various critical functions.

(D) *Socio-political inquiries about societies under law*

Writers on jurisprudence may set themselves questions like: 'What is there in common between the governmental organizations and/or the social structures to be found in societies in which there exists that institutional complex commonly referred to as a "legal system"?'

In particular, they may conduct such inquiries about the judicial process, the central institutional activity of developed legal systems. General jurisprudence may look for universal rationalistic or psychological elements in the fact-finding process or in the procedures of argument before courts. In this book, we confine ourselves to elements in the judicial process which are common to it and to the law-stating and law-criticizing functions of legal science as a whole. In particular, we investigate the models of rationality which are employed by courts in justification of legal decisions, where the values of legality and constitutionality allow more than one decision to be made.

'Shared understandings' are probably a feature of all institutions;[1] and, in the case of modern legal institutions, these shared understandings include the logic of legal science. It follows that a comprehensive socio-political study of institutions, such as courts, legislatures, prosecution offices, and the police, ought to include the traditional questions of jurisprudence.

This is particularly true where the object of study is courts of justice. The values of legality and constitutionality play some part in the roles of all officials, so that the logic of descriptive legal science is material to every state institution. But in the case of courts, the administration of 'justice according to law' requires (as I shall argue) not merely acceptance of these values, but also the application of some combination of the legal models of rationality to doubtful cases. One of the most important of these models of rationality, the doctrine model, can only be understood in the light of an explication of the conception of historic legal system. Thus, to get a complete picture of any state institution, one must take on the conception of 'law' as rules, and to understand courts, one must add the conception of 'law' as doctrine.

Nevertheless, much more than traditional jurisprudential

---

[1] Cf. A. M. Honoré: 'Groups, Laws and Obedience', *O.E.J.*, p. 1.

inquiries can offer would be needed for a complete institutional portrait. When jurisprudential writers concern themselves with macroscopic questions about aspects of societies under law other than the functioning of courts, their conclusions tend to be distorted by their preoccupation with the specifically 'legal' aspects of such societies. In other words, when they are supposed to be discussing universals about 'legal systems', in the sense of institutional structures, they tend to over-emphasize 'legal systems', in the sense of normative fields of meaning, or 'legal systems', in the sense of collections of doctrine. What is universal (if anything) about the structure and validity of the two latter conceptions will be among the features, but by no means the most important feature, of the former.

I shall consider some attempts made by certain jurisprudential writers to answer this kind of macroscopic question about political societies. This will be done only in order to explain some of the reasons which impelled these writers to adopt particular theorems about the concepts legal rule and legal system. I shall not attempt to improve very much on their answers. Such answers may be compared with the conclusions about the same kind of questions reached by writers on political theory or social structure who do not share the specifically legal preoccupation to which we have just referred, preferring (perhaps) some other specialist bias.

II

Theories of Law

Theorems (*a*) *to* (*k*)

(a) A positive legal rule is to be equated with the expression of an act of wishing.

(b) A legal system is to be equated with all the positive legal rules emanating from the same sovereign will.

(c) A positive legal rule is to be equated with a 'pure norm', that is, with an *ought* or *may* meaning-content.

(d) A legal system is to be equated with a collection of pure norms interpreted by legal scientists as a non-contradictory field of meaning—such interpretation entailing the logical postulate that legal norms must originate in a finite number of sources.

(e) A positive legal rule is to be equated with a 'rule-idea', that is, with the psychological occurrence represented by an internalized normative assertion about behaviour, coupled with a (positive or negative) imperative stimulus.

(f) A legal system is to be equated with the mass of rule-ideas, intermittently revived in the minds of the members of a political community, which owe their psychological effectiveness to the echo of certain law-words.

(g) A legal system is to be equated with the sum total of rule-ideas which (predictably) will influence the verbal behaviour of the officials in a political community.

(h) A positive legal rule is to be equated with a 'rule-situation', that is, with a social situation in which a certain pattern of behaviour is regarded as a standard.

(i)   A legal system is to be equated with a social situation in which obligation-standards—that is, standards enforced by strong social pressure—are generally observed, and the officials of the society agree as to which patterns of behaviour are relevant to the creation of new obligation-standards.

(j)   A positive legal rule is to be equated with a 'paper rule', that is, a written assertion which can be used for guiding or justifying choices.

(k)   A legal system is to be equated with a congeries of paper rules, and other choice-guidance/justification devices such as principles, policies, and maxims, available for the use of officials in settling disputes.

4.   THE WILL THEORY OF LAW

(A)   *Unity of enforcement entails unity of will*

Theorems (a) and (b), set out above, are implicit in the writings of Jeremy Bentham and John Austin, the founders in England of positivist jurisprudence. Bentham's principal definition avoids the concept legal rule altogether:

'A law may be defined as an assemblage of signs declarative of a volition conceived or adopted by the *sovereign* in a state, concerning the conduct to be observed in a certain *case* by a certain person or class of persons . . .'[1]

In principle, according to Bentham, every act stipulated by law is so stipulated because it is the object of the sovereign's will, and not because it is required or permitted by some intervening entity called 'a rule'. The 'sovereign's will', however, here means the sovereign's *full will*, his will as bloated by the absorption of inferior wills. In Bentham's view, the sovereign adopts as his own all orders which he does not prohibit.[2] The mandates of the master, father, husband, guardian are as much the mandates of the sovereign as are those of the general or judge. The proof of this lies in the fact that: 'in one case as well as in another the business of enforcing them must rest ultimately with the sovereign'.[3]

---

[1] *O.L.G.*, p. 1.   [2] *O.L.G.*, p. 3.

[3] *O.L.G.*, pp. 22–3. Bentham overlooked the possibility that the sovereign might enforce the contents of commands even though he prohibited the act of command-

A 'complete' law may only be achieved through the co-operation of a sovereign legislator and one or more subordinates. The legislator issues a 'general' law that defines the acts which are its 'objects' and the persons and things which are its 'subjects' by class names. The general law is completed when a subordinate, by the exercise of 'accensitive power', fills out these classes with individual acts, persons, and things.[1] A law is completely enacted only when the words constituting it are so precise that it may be applied merely with the help of a dictionary.[2]

Hence, the words in Bentham's definition are to be understood in the following way. 'Conduct in a certain case' is intended to indicate an individual action: and 'person or class of persons' is intended to indicate that, either the person bound by a complete law is a specified individual, or that the persons so bound are a class whose indeterminacy relates to number and not to qualities common to them all which are capable of further individuation.

Bentham gives the following example of a complete law: 'Let no one, Rusticus excepted (so we will call the proprietor), "and those whom he allows meddle with such or such a field".'[3]

One might object that the act prohibited in this example is not in fact completely individuated. Lawyers might debate endlessly, in and out of court, whether certain borderline kinds of conduct amounted to 'meddling with' and reference to the dictionary might not help. Very often the object of a 'complete' law cannot be a fully individuated act—and thus a 'conduct in a certain case', in Bentham's sense—until after it has been adjudged such by one of the sovereign's subordinates.

The generalized form of this objection is that: if a law is identified with what is (fully) willed, and if what is willed is identified with what is enforced, the conduct stipulated by laws can never be known in advance of enforcement. If the law is supposed to address the citizen about his action before he acts so that he can choose obedience or disobedience—and Bentham certainly thought this was so—we need some notion of what

---

ing, and vice versa—cf. H. L. A. Hart: 'Bentham on Legal Powers' (1972), 81 Y.L.J. 799. In other words, he failed to distinguish acts which are legally permitted from those which, by virtue of a subsumptive relation, are legally authorized—cf. *infra.* p. 86.

[1] *O.L.G.*, pp. 80–5. [2] *O.L.G.*, pp. 158–9. [3] *O.L.G.*, p. 177.

sort of thing the law requires as an idea intervening between acts of legislation and enforcement. The form of this ideational content is supplied by the conception of a legal rule. In terms of this conception, the principle of subsumption takes the place of Bentham's absorption of inferior wills.

For example, according to Bentham, if the sovereign allows to any citizen a power of choosing what persons, things, or actions are to come within general classes specified in the sovereign's legislation, the law is not complete until such 'accensitive power' has been exercised. A property law created by a conveyance is thus the joint product of the legislator and the person executing the conveyance.[1] The logic of legal science requires no such complex unit. A general law prohibiting 'meddling with' land is a complete positive legal rule if it is contained in legislative source-materials; and, by virtue of conditions of title incorporated in it, the particular rule about Rusticus is subsumable under it.[2] No will-absorption is required.

In fact Bentham only dispenses with the conception of legal rule as a matter of socio-political analysis. Like many other theorists, he elides the third and fourth tasks of general jurisprudence mentioned in the last chapter. He offers us the meddling-with-field example as a model into which all legislative material and all lawful commands could be forced, and thus (in his view) demonstrates the supreme importance for understanding political society of the units 'sovereign power' and 'sovereign will'.

Bentham fully realized the practical importance of the concept *legal rule* to the analysis of 'legislation'. He recognized that what the legislator enacts, and what legal science deals with, are 'general laws', specifying acts and persons by non-individuated, class descriptions.[3] As a code-maker, he sought to achieve the best general rules which (through the motivation they would exercise) would have the best consequences in terms of general happiness.

Bentham's follower, John Austin, used the terms 'law' and 'rule' interchangeably. Like Bentham he regarded rules ('general commands') as intimations of wishes or desires, and

---

[1] *O.L.G.*, pp. 179–81.   [2] See *infra*, p. 84.   [3] *O.L.G.*, pp. 81, 174–5.

equated the law of a community with the totality of the sovereign's expressed wishes.[1]

Of the many respects in which his definition of law differs
from Bentham's, two are especially indicative of a difference in
jurisprudential aim. First, he limited laws to commands
which oblige 'generally to acts or forbearances of a class'.[2]
Second, he designated as 'circuitous commands' of the sovereign, and hence as laws, only those general commands of
citizens which are made 'in pursuance of legal rights';[3] which
encompasses only commands with a fiduciary element, such as
those of a guardian to his ward and not those made for the
commander's own benefit, such as those of a master to his
servant.[4]

It seems that, in defining 'a law', Austin was not content
simply to arrive at a model which would exemplify the units of
power and will. He wanted his definition to serve the purpose
of defining the province of jurisprudence. That is to say, he
wanted the definition to include only those sorts of orders issued
(or tolerated and enforced) by the sovereign which are the stuff
of the lawyer's trade. Only when the acts commanded by the
sovereign are general, will anything worth discussion by legal
scientists have been added to the body of the laws. The mandates of the master and the father might be related (through
enforcement) to the sovereign in the same way as the orders of
the general or of the judge, but no one would ever write legal
textbooks about their contents, and analysis of their specific
terminology was of no special legal interest.

Yet, despite these qualifications, Austin, like Bentham, believed that the sovereign willed all 'laws', whatever their immediate source. And his justification for the assumption of unity of
will is the same, namely, unity of enforcement. He says, for
example, that the state's 'sovereign will' that judge-made rules

---

[1] *P.J.D.*, pp. 17, 254–7, 358–61. However, whereas Austin supposed that the
sovereign's power to command *must* extend to all areas of life, Bentham's view was
that there might be limits to a sovereign's legislative power set by the population's
disposition to obey (*O.L.G.*, pp. 18–20). Cf. H. L. A. Hart: 'Bentham on
Sovereignty' (1967), Irish Jurist 327. Hart argues, in effect, that, although over a
period of time there must be a correlation between what can in practice be enforced and the possession of legislative power, at any one moment of time the limits
of legislative power are conceived by legal scientists (including legal officials) in
terms of constitutional source-rules. Cf. *infra*, p. 74.

[2] *P.J.D.*, p. 19.   [3] *P.J.D.*, p. 134.   [4] *P.J.D.*, p. 137, n.

'shall obtain as law' is evinced by the fact that it permits the judge to enforce them 'by the power of the political community'.[1]

The same is true, according to Austin and Bentham, of the laws originating from sovereigns who formerly received habitual obedience. Their wills are absorbed in the will of the sovereign person or body who now enforces what they willed.[2]

Thus both writers equate that entity which (under the description 'legal rule') is issued and repealed by legislatures and is the subject-matter of legal science, with words or other signs expressing an act of wishing ('volition', 'wish or desire') (Theorem (a)). Both equate the legal system, in the sense of all the legal rules valid at any moment of time in a society, with the totality of legal rules emanating from the same sovereign will (Theorem (b)). That legal rules emanate from the sovereign's will follows from the fact that he enforces them. Unity of enforcement entails unity of will.

(B) *The value of sovereign will as a constructive metaphor*

Enough has been said to demonstrate just how thoroughgoing was the will theory to which these early positivist writers committed themselves. Bentham and Austin stigmatized traditional natural law theory for its failure to distinguish law as it is from law as it ought to be. Positive laws, they said, must be defined, not in terms of values, but in terms of facts.[3] But the facts they offer turn out to be acts of wishing on the part of certain politically powerful individuals supposedly to be found in every society. In the case, not just of some laws, but of every law that is valid at any one time in a society, the persons who are for the moment sovereign in that society have a wish directed towards its content.

A familiar objection to identifying a positive legal rule with the expression of a sovereign will is that, if 'sovereign will' is understood in a psychological sense, no such will actually exists so far as the bulk of legislation in a modern state is concerned. It is impossible to identify any act of wishing by which a legislative body consciously rewills the wishes of previous sovereigns, or of past judges. Nor are there any such spasms of wishing

---

[1] *P.J.D.*, pp. 31–2.   [2] *P.J.D.*, p. 193; *O.L.G.*, pp. 21–2.
[3] Bentham: *A Fragment on Government* (W. Harrison, ed.), 1960, pp. 7–8. *P.J.D.*, pp. 184–5.

directed to the contents of laws to be issued in the future by subordinate powerholders. It is also difficult to see in what sense a legislative body, as a body, consciously addresses itself (volitionally) to the contents of a bill. Clearly the members who vote against do not do so; and it is a contingent circumstance whether or not the majority *wish* the directive materials contained in the bill, or whether they simply *wish to vote* for some other reason. In the case of an obscure section in a taxing statute, it may be that only the bosom of the draftsman ever heaved volitionally towards what it prescribes.

If Bentham and Austin really intended to define laws in terms of psychological acts of wishing, it is astonishing that they nowhere offered counter-arguments to the above empirical objections. Can it be then that, despite their use of psychological-looking expressions like 'conceiving a volition' and 'conceiving a wish or desire', they intended to describe acts of wishing in some non-psychological sense?

One explanation which might be advanced is that they accepted the metaphysic of the will. To the philosophic tradition which conceives of mental processes in a trinity of thought, feeling and will, there is nothing surprising in attributing to the will the features which Bentham and Austin ascribed to the sovereign will. According to the metaphysic, the 'will' is not to be identified with any one, or any series, of psychological acts of wishing. It can operate without the consciousness of its human host. It can also splice itself with other wills into the general will of a legislative body or of any other group.

If the sovereign will is a metaphysical entity, there is nothing odd in ascribing to it the power to absorb the wills of earlier sovereigns and of subordinate powerholders. There is, indeed, nothing odd—apart from the oddness of the metaphysical conception itself—in ascribing to the sovereign will anything which the law stipulates.

Can it be that, in the hands of these theorists, the state, being shorn of other divine qualities, yet retains the divine quality of omnivolence? If all that occurs is willed by God, there is an entailment between the assertion that something has occurred and that God willed it. If we transfer the transcendental and omnivolent qualities of the divine will to the will of the sovereign in a state, it becomes possible to create an entailment between the assertion that a particular rule is enforced by the sovereign and the assertion that the sovereign wills the rule. The existence of this entailment between enforcement and will would explain why Bentham and Austin offered no empirical proof that the persons who wield power actually will the laws.[1]

In connection with their definitions of a law, Bentham and Austin speak the language of a will metaphysic. But there is evidence from other parts of their writings—in different contexts—that they did not believe in it. Bentham ridiculed Blackstone's assertion that all the subjects of a state form a (non-natural) political union out of their separate private wills, by pointing out that in fact no one submits his will; and he regarded Blackstone's assumption that a governing body can be taken to have one common will as illegitimate, although, in the context of his own definitions, this is an assumption which he himself makes.[2] Austin, when discussing the difference between intentional and negligent acts, says that the so-called 'will' underlying specific volitions is 'just nothing at all'.[3]

The most charitable explanation of this paradox is that Bentham and Austin made use of this convenient and familiar metaphysical language as a constructive metaphor. Political power was organized behind the directives of the law *as if* the sovereign were willing them all. Although they were perfectly well aware that the sovereign cannot wish all the contents of all the laws in a psychological sense, and although they did not accept that there was some other (non-natural) sense in which one can conceive volitions, they none the less thought it profitable, as part of their macroscopic analysis of political societies,

[1] For Austin, the expressions of God's will and the expressions of the will of political superiors were both species of the same *genus*, 'commands'—*P.J.D.*, p. 33 ff. Bentham, having asserted that all lawful mandates, however trivial, were mandates of the sovereign (*O.L.G.*, pp. 22–3), added a marginal note to his manuscript as follows: 'To deny it is as much as to say that it is God Almighty indeed that keeps up the race of elephants, but it is somebody else who keeps up the race of mites.' This sentence appears in the first published version of *Of Laws in General—The Limits of Jurisprudence Defined*, 1945, p. 105—but is omitted from the later edition since Bentham had heavily deleted it in pencil. (For this information I am indebted to Professor Hart.) Bentham gives us no alternative reason why the willing of trivial commands by the sovereign cannot be denied.

[2] *A Fragment on Government* (W. Harrison, ed.), 1960, pp. 87–8, 90–1.

[3] J. Austin: *Lectures on Jurisprudence*, 5th edn. (R. Campbell, ed.), 1885, vol. i, p. 412.

to employ the conception of a sovereign will directed towards all rules which are enforced in a state. There is no direct authority for this suggestion in their writings. Over-all jurisprudential aim is something about which the greatest theorists are often unhappily silent. The ground for the suggestion is the fact that any other interpretation attributes to these authors either fantastic empirical assumptions, or grotesque inconsistency.

As a constructive metaphor, *sovereign will* would have value in political theory, if it illuminated or pointed up the ways in which political societies actually work. As such it is somewhat crude. Even if we allow that it is of the essence of positive laws that they are all enforced by state coercion, a concept which identifies the coercing 'state' with the individuals who (for the time being) constitute the legislature casts more darkness than light. It is one of the aims of political theory to provide models which give insights into the roles and institutions of those who actually get their way in political societies, and certainly coercion ought to have a place in such models. But those who compose the legislature need only (by virtue of their typical roles) vote laws. Many of them may not get their way about very much, and their institutional relationship to the exercise of state coercion varies enormously from society to society—which shows that it is not dependent on their role as legislators.[1]

There is, however, another justification for the concept *sovereign will* of which Bentham at least was aware. It can be understood as a concept, not of political, but of legal theory. As such it would not purport to point up anything illuminating about political society as a whole, but only about the discipline of legal science.

Legal scientists characteristically insist on interpreting the legislative material of a state as a non-contradictory field of meaning. In other words, when faced with two normative stipu-

[1] Recognizing this, J. C. Gray sought to improve on the conception of Austinian sovereignty by identifying as the true authors of positive law the 'real rulers of society'—a faceless cartel, standing behind the legislature and the courts, who manipulate the institutions of the state in their own interests—*The Nature and Sources of the Law*, 2nd edn., 1921, pp. 67–9. In fact, both legislature and 'real rulers' (if they exist) are authors of law, bearing in mind the different sense of 'legal system' distinguished in the last chapter. The former is one of the sources from which the rules constituting the present law originate. The latter are the sustainers of the complex of legal institutions.

lations which direct contradictory behaviour, they generally insist either that there is no real contradiction, or that the 'validity' of one entails the 'invalidity' of the other.

Now what is the logical justification for such a practice? It cannot be the same as the logical justification for denying contradictions in an assertive field of meaning, because it does not bear the same relation to 'truth', or to what actually may be the case. Classical logic takes as an axiom that one cannot assert both that it is the case that (x) and also that it is not the case that (x). Roughly, if what is meant by 'is the case' is some relation to empirical reality, the truth-ground of this axiom arises from the widely accepted assumption that the physical manifestations of nature are not an illusion. Granted this assumption, if it is really true that (x) is the case, it cannot be really true that (x) is not the case. A normative field of meaning, on the other hand does not speak of what is the case, but of what ought to be done. The legal-science principle of non-contradiction cannot be justified by reference to the assumed non-illusoriness of nature. To discover a justification for axioms of this sort is one of the problems faced in the recent development of 'deontic logic'—the logic of *must, must not,* and *may* propositions. The best equivalent truth-ground which one of its leading exponents has been able to find is the presupposition of a rational will underlying all the norms of a consistent system of norms. If, when we make assertions about what ought to be done, we assume as a postulate that we are talking about the kind of instructions which could be given by a person with a rational will, the postulate justifies us in saying that contradictory actions cannot be directed. A rational person could not knowingly order an individual to perform an act on a particular occasion and at the same time excuse or prohibit him from performing it.[1]

Bentham foresaw the need for such a 'logic of the will'.[2] For him the assumption of a united sovereign will standing behind all the laws does for legal science what the assumption of a truth-ground does for the natural sciences: it provides a basis for the four principles of the logic of legal science set out in the last chapter. It justifies the principle of non-contradiction, since laws issued 'uno flatu' by the legislator cannot be totally repug-

[1] *N.A.*, pp. 147–52, 203–7.   [2] *I.P.M.*, pp. 8–9; *O.L.G.*, p. 15.

nant;[1] the principle of derogation, since the sovereign must intend his 'primordial' mandates to give way before his later 'superventitious' mandates;[2] and the principle of subsumption, since mandates emanating from other persons' wills are laws by virtue of their adoption by the sovereign, either in advance ('pre-adoption'), or retrospectively ('susception').[3] Bentham's equivalent of the principle of exclusion is his 'universal law of liberty', according to which all acts not prohibited by the sovereign are permitted.[4]

As a conception of political theory, 'sovereign will' is of little value; but as a conception of legal theory intended simply to explain the logical basis of descriptive legal science, it has much in its favour. Later in this book, reasons are given for preferring the alternative of a presupposed 'basic legal science fiat'. They have to do with the fact that the chief practical consequence of the inarticulate will theory which does in fact underlie some legal science is the undue emphasis it gives to the will model of rationality as a guide to legal development.

5. THE PURE-NORM THEORY OF LAW

(A) *Norm, ought, and will*

Theorems (c) and (d), set out at the beginning of this chapter, are intended to extract the distinctive definitional core of the legal theory of Hans Kelsen. Despite fluctuations in his views on many other points, Kelsen maintained for half a century the theory that law is pure norm. One of his leading themes was the demonstration that legal rules are abstract entities identifiable neither with the events which give rise to them (their legislative history), nor with the events which constitute their application (judicial or administrative enforcement); and that the sort of abstract entity which they constitute is normative meaning-content.[5]

On this major point, it will be argued, Kelsen was right. Statements in legal science about existing (valid) rules cannot, without change of meaning, be reinterpreted as statements

---

[1] *O.L.G.*, pp. 125–6.   [2] *O.L.G.*, pp. 93–132.   [3] *O.L.G.*, pp. 21–9.
[4] *O.L.G.*, pp. 119–20.
[5] *G.T.*, pp. 30–7; *W.J.*, pp. 267–74; *P.T.L.*, pp. 85–9, 101–7; *E.L.M.P.*, pp. 216–27.

about the past behaviour of legislatures or the future behaviour of officials, or any other events. Any attempt so to reinterpret them would result in a 'change of meaning', because—as I shall try to show—the logical procedures and values at present operative in descriptive legal science are applicable only to rules, and indeed only to rules in the pure-norm sense. As Kelsen writes: 'The legal statements that one ought to behave in a certain way cannot be reduced to statements about present or future facts, because the former do not refer to such facts, not even to the fact that certain individuals wish that one ought to behave in a certain way.'[1]

Unfortunately, Kelsen failed to make it clear that laws are pure norms simply because it is the practice of legal scientists (including legal officials) to treat them as such. In other words, the pure-norm theory of law is not about 'law', but about that pervasive institutional discipline, the practice of legal science. He begins his inquiry into 'the definition of law' by asking: what social order is referred to by common usage of the word 'law' and its equivalents in other languages?[2] He thus denies himself the possibility of pointing out that 'law', as the subject-matter of legal science, is not necessarily the same thing as is referred to in other disciplines by use of the word 'law'. He claims, as we mentioned in the last chapter, that his pure theory explains the intellectual processes of legal science,[3] but does not recognize that that is all that it explains. Further, he has a very restrictive view of those processes: '. . . the task of the science of law is not to approve or disapprove its subject, but to know and describe it'.[4] He assumes, wrongly, that description is the only proper activity of legal science.

The units of meaning-content into which legal science divides its subject-matter, Kelsen calls 'norms'. He preferred the word 'norm' to the word 'rule' for two reasons.[5] First, he feared that use of the term 'rule' might lead to confusion with the natural sciences. This is not the case in English, where, if anything, the word 'law' is more ambiguous in this respect. In English, the word 'norm' has its own special ambiguity, since it is used in the social sciences to describe 'rule-situations' considered in section 7 of this chapter. Second, Kelsen thought, the word 'rule' was

[1] *P.T.L.*, p. 104.   [2] *G.T.*, p. 4; *W.J.*, p. 266; *P.T.L.*, p. 30.   [3] *Supra*, p. 19.
[4] *P.T.L.*, p. 68.   [5] *G.T.*, pp. 37–8.

not apt to cover the case of a particular norm directing a single act unconditionally. This is correct. However, the positive legal rules/norms which legal science describes are seldom of this unconditional kind, so that we are justified in employing the more familiar term. Kelsen himself throughout his theory, lays the greatest stress on general norms.[1]

Such terminological questions are of little significance. Much more important is the off-key note given to his entire theory by Kelsen's increasing preoccupation with the reification (the 'thinginess') of norms. He was not content to say that the legal rules/norms which are the subject-matter of descriptive legal science are normative propositions whose nature is exclusively a function of the discipline which uses them. Instead, he sought to show that 'norms' were bits of meaning-content with a life of their own—a moment of birth, a distinctive ontology, and a thing-like integrity (so that their destruction could result only from human choice, and not from logical operations). This is a pointless project. There is no point in a 'theory of norms' distinct from a theory of normative propositions which are or could be used in performing intellectual operations. Kelsen's preoccupation with norms as meaning-content-objects led him into difficulties, as will be argued in later chapters, in connection with the conception of validity and with the working of the principles of derogation and non-contradiction. It also led him into strange entanglements of the three concepts *norm*, *ought*, and *will*.

In his *General Theory of Law and State*, Kelsen defined a 'norm' as 'the expression of the idea . . . that an individual ought to behave in a certain way'.[2] 'Ought' was a symbol standing for a special class of vocabulary used to create norms. This *ought* category of language was not defined, except by being contrasted with the *is* category. Kelsen persistently attempted to tie in his view that rules of law are abstract entities, distinct from past legislation or future application, with the widely accepted Humean principle that a valid syllogism cannot be constructed in which the major and minor premises are both expressed in terms of *is*, whilst the conclusion is expressed as an *ought*.[3]

---

[1] *G.T.*, p. 124 ff; *P.T.L.*, p. 230 ff.   [2] *G.T.*, p. 36.
[3] *G.T.*, pp. 110–12; *P.T.L.*, pp. 6, 193–5; *E.L.M.P.*, pp. 217, 219.

This attempt to found the nature of legal rules on the logical cleavage between *is* and *ought* is unhelpful because, as Kelsen himself came to recognize, words do not on their face indicate to which category an assertion belongs.[1] Legislative source-materials do not employ a specialized kind of verb or gram-matical mood, patently distinguishable from the verb-forms and moods used in descriptive discourse. So far as language is concerned, there is no sharp line between an *is* category and an *ought* category.

It is perhaps for this reason that, in his later works, Kelsen endeavoured to specify the nature of the legal *ought* in some way other than by simply contrasting it with *is*. 'As a "norm" the law is the specific meaning of an act of will directed at a definite human behaviour. This meaning is: that men ought to behave in a certain way.'[2]

Thus norms are defined in terms, not of the use of a special normative vocabulary, but of the performance of a special kind of act; and the nature of 'ought' changes from being a symbolic representation of normative language to being a symbolic representation of semantic function. Norms are, by definition, the meaning-contents which acts of will express; and 'ought' is, by stipulation, the appropriate word to represent this type of meaning—Kelsen was aware that 'in customary usage' words like 'ought' might be used in many different ways.[3]

Thus, if I say: 'you will do this', from my words alone it does not appear whether I am making a prediction or issuing a com-mand. But if from the context you know that I am commanding, then you know that the meaning of what I say is not to be ascribed to the indicative mood, but is the sort of meaning which could be interpreted ('objectively') as a valid norm. Similarly, by noting whether or not a legislator was expressing an act of will, we are able to tell whether the material he pro-duced is 'normative'—that is, (1) creative of norms, and (2) such that we can transcribe its meaning in terms of the stipu-lated 'ought'.[4]

Kelsen's later view of 'ought' as 'meaning of act of will' led

[1] *E.L.M.P.*, pp. 274–5. Cf. *N.A.*, pp. 96–8, 100–3; and *D.N.*, pp. 69–74.
[2] 'On the Pure Theory of Law' (1966), 1 Israel L.R. 1.
[3] *E.L.M.P.*, p. 224.
[4] *P.T.L.*, pp. 4–10; *E.L.M.P.*, pp. 217–18, 229–30.

him to reject his own earlier arguments about the creation of norms. He was formerly of the opinion that statute law could not be said to be created by an act of will of the majority of the legislature, and that customary law was not created by anybody's acts of will.[1] Both of these opinions he subsequently repudiated.[2]

These renunciations were unnecessary. We can accept Kelsen's characterization of legal rules as 'meanings of acts of will', in this sense: rules of law have the same logical force that commands directed at the same act-situation would have, so that the language of 'compliance' or 'obedience' is equally appropriate to both. The 'ought' of a rule stipulating: 'courts (in circumstances x) ought to award damages', has the same deontic role as it would have had if these words had been commanded by a king. But we are not thereby committed to saying that any particular individual 'willed' the rule in question. From the standpoint of the commanded, laws do share characteristics with commands; but they are quite different when looked at from the other end of the gun. As logical units, legal rules and meanings of commands can be classed together; as 'speech performatives', they have nothing in common.

Further, we can accept a stipulation that 'ought' shall stand for the mandatory deontic operator within legal rules, without being committed to any particular view of the *is-ought* cleavage; and, of course, the acceptance of such a stipulative 'ought' is not inconsistent with a recognition that, in ordinary usage, the word 'ought' is not a synonym for words like 'shall', 'must', 'is required to' and the like.[3]

The reason why words in legislative materials which may be grammatically ambiguous are interpreted as normative is not because, in the context, we know that the legislators (or any of them) underwent a volitional act. It is because the words were contained in legislative materials. It is as much the characteristic function of the legislature to enact stipulations as it is the function of legal science to construct the law out of these materials. In the context of ambiguous speech-acts, the only way to find out whether the mood expressed is imperative or indicative

[1] *G.T.*, pp. 33–5; *W.J.*, p. 273.   [2] *S.L.R.*, pp. 1138–9; *P.T.L.*, pp. 9, 226.
[3] Cf. D. N. MacCormick: 'Legal Obligation and the Imperative Fallacy', *O.E.J.*, p. 100.

is to ask: what grounds are there for thinking that the speaker is expressing a wish rather than making a statement?[1] In the context of legislation, such a question would be out of place. Whether or not any particular individual willed any part of the law, all legislators legislate rather than describe. (It may be, as we shall see in chapter five, in place to ask *why* particular individuals wished to legislate.)

Kelsen's flirtation with will theory led him into special difficulties in connection with his doctrine of the 'basic norm'. As we shall see, the basic norm is presupposed by legal science because legal science accepts only certain sources as law-creating, these sources being stipulated by the basic norm of each legal system. Now because the basic norm is a norm it must, Kelsen decided, not only be 'the meaning of an act of will' in the sense which I have described as acceptable, but must also have an actual will as its counterpart. Since, however, it is a presupposed and not a positive norm, Kelsen was forced to attach this cornerstone of his theory to an 'imaginary' will.[2]

The part which will-theory played in Kelsen's later work may be summed up in four propositions: (1) All norms are the meanings of acts of will, that is their logical nature. (2) All norms but one in a national legal order are created by real acts of will. (3) The basic norm of a national legal order is presupposed in any statement of legal science made about that national legal order. (4) When the basic norm is presupposed, its logical form as a norm means that an act of will of which it is the content must be being imagined.

As has been said, the first of these propositions is acceptable, provided it is understood as relating only to the logical category into which norms fall, not to any assumptions about actual willings. I shall also give reasons for accepting the third proposition, in a modified form. The second and fourth are mistakes. They result from Kelsen's tendency to reify norms, which impels him to confer a moment of creation on each positive norm. A legal rule, in the pure-norm sense, is a normative proposition, affirmed by some statement in legal science to be

[1] Whether the 'illocution' in question is appropriately described as a 'command' or 'order', as opposed to a 'plea', 'request', or 'prayer', will turn on whether there is the assumption of superiority which conventionally distinguishes imperatives from other wish-expressions—cf. MacCormick: *O.E.J.*, pp. 102–9.

[2] *P.T.L.*, pp. 9–10; *E.L.M.P.*, p. 220.

part of the present law. Its source may consist of a datable, single act of legislation, but often this is not the case.

Kelsen changed his view not only on the nature of ought, but also on its semantic status. In his earlier writings, the meaning conveyed by the 'ought' of every norm was the same as that conveyed by the imperative mood in conventional grammars. Norms were 'depsychologized commands'.[1] In his later writings, the unity of *ought* was replaced by a trinity of *ought*, *may*, and *can*. Norms became 'commands', 'permissions', or 'authorizations'.[2] At the same time Kelsen was anxious to preserve the *ought* as a unified category, in order to maintain the duality between it and the *is* category. He therefore continued to describe all norms in terms of *ought*, whilst admitting that, by using it to cover permissions and authorizations as well as commands, he was employing the word 'ought' in a broader sense than usage accords to it.[3]

It seems to me that the last member of the trinity is superfluous, and that legal rules have at most two deontic operators, namely, *ought*, and *may*.[4] According to Kelsen's later view, a norm requiring or permitting a judge to impose a fine would have to be categorized as an 'authorization', because what it requires/permits (the imposition of the fine) itself creates a further norm: and 'to authorize' means 'to confer the power to create law'.[5] As I shall argue in the next chapter,[6] however, the higher norm does not have a function of 'authorization' distinct from its function of 'command' or 'permission' directed towards the judicial action which created the lower norm. The relation between the norms is not inherent in the higher norm, but is created by legal science itself pursuant to the principle of subsumption.

Kelsen eventually differentiated four types of norms corresponding to four supposedly distinct normative functions: commands, permissions, authorizations, and derogating norms.[7] We consider in the next chapter the general question of taxonomy by reference to function.[8] For the moment it is enough to say that the possibility of subsumptive relations between norms is

[1] *G.T.*, p. 35; *W.J.*, p. 273.   [2] *P.T.L.*, pp. 5, 74.
[3] *P.T.L.*, pp. 6, 10, 77, 119.
[4] Cf. *J.W.*, Harris: 'Kelsen's Concept of Authority' (1977), 36 *C.L.J.*, 353
[5] *P.T.L.*, p. 115.   [6] *Infra*, p. 87.   [7] *E.L.M.P.*, pp. 216, 234, 261.   [8] *Infra*, p. 98.

no sufficient reason for introducing a distinct authorizing deontic operator. Hence Theorem (c) equates a positive legal rule with an ought or may meaning-content.

(B) *The basic norm and the principle of exclusion*

We have seen how, in explaining the concept *legal rule*, Kelsen's point of departure was the impossibility of translating into statements of fact legal statements to the effect that one ought to behave in a certain way. Similarly, in explaining the concept *legal system*, he focused on the descriptive epithets which legal science may apply to conduct—such as 'legal', 'illegal', 'an offence', etc.—and sought to show their epistemological bases. Part of his conclusion was that legal science insists on interpreting the meaning-contents contained in source materials as a non-contradictory unity. In so far as the law on any topic is clear, what it stipulates cannot be contradicted by any valid norm within it.[1]

. . . (S)ince the cognition of law, like any cognition, seeks to understand its subject as a meaningful whole and to describe it in non-contradictory statements, it starts from the assumption that conflicts of norms within the normative order which is the object of this cognition can and must be solved by interpretation.[2]

As indicated in the first part of Theorem (d), Kelsen's partial conclusion is that a legal system is to be equated with a collection of pure norms interpreted by legal scientists as a non-contradictory field of meaning. Lawyers come to their work already armed with the principles of derogation and non-contradiction. (In the next chapter, we consider a different view taken about these principles in essays published during the last decade of Kelsen's life.)[3]

But the principles of derogation and non-contradiction could not be enough to explain the sense in which legal science systematizes rules. Two persons engaged in a moral debate might agree to apply these principles within their discussion, and yet disagree on every point of moral duty. This could happen if they had different views of what was to count as sources

[1] *G.T.*, p. 437; *W.J.*, pp. 280, 284; 'What is the Pure Theory of Law?' (1959–60), 34 Tulane L.R. 269, 271; *S.L.R.*, p. 1143; *P.T.L.*, pp. 74, 206.
[2] *P.T.L.*, p. 206. [3] *E.L.M.P.*, chs. 9–13.

of moral rules. Discussions about the existing law on a topic are not *at large* in the same way. The categorical assertions about legality which legal science makes take the form they do only because descriptive legal-science discourse postulates that legal rules must either themselves originate in a finite number of sources, or else be related (pursuant to the principle of subsumption) to such source-rules.

The existence of what was termed in the last chapter 'the principle of exclusion' is the foundation of Kelsen's famous doctrine of the basic norm. The basic norm requires that only certain sources shall count as ultimate legislative sources. It is the equivalent of the constructive metaphor of a sovereign will, a 'presupposition' or 'hypothesis' of legal science.[1]

However, his various formulations of the basic norm show that by it Kelsen intended to do more than merely make explicit the principle of exclusion. He sought to exemplify a particular theory of constitutional continuity.

'. . . [C]oercive acts ought to be carried out only under the conditions and in the way determined by the "fathers" of the constitution or the organs delegated by them.'[2]

'Coercion of man against man ought to be exercised in the manner and under the conditions determined by the historically first constitution.'[3]

In terms of such formulations, the legal system at whose apex a basic norm stands may be understood to comprise all those norms originating over a period of time from a constitution promulgated at a certain historical date, including constitutionally-enacted changes in the constitution;[4] and the system changes always when, and only when, a breach in constitutional continuity occurs.[5] French law of today is consequently within the same system as every law valid in France since that breach in constitutional continuity which inaugurated the Fifth Republic in 1958, since all such norms would be subsumable under that basic norm which validates the constitution then promulgated.

But, whatever may be the 'legal system' which comprises a

---

[1] *G.T.*, pp. 117, 396, 437; *P.T.L.*, p. 204; *S.L.R.*, pp. 1144, 1149.
[2] *G.T.*, p. 116.   [3] *P.T.L.*, p. 50.
[4] Cf. Alf Ross: 'On Self-reference and a Puzzle in Constitutional Law' (1969), 78 *Mind* 1.   [5] See *infra*, p. 80.

country's past as well as its present law, it is not that non-contradictory field of meaning—the present law—in terms of which categorical statements about legality are made. There is, indeed, no such conception of legal system peculiar to legal science, although it may form the subject-matter of historical judgments of a political or ethical kind—'Our law has always supported private property', 'Our law is becoming increasingly humane'. Demarcation criteria presupposed in such judgments will be heavily context-dependent; they are unlikely to coincide with those suggested by any theory of constitutional continuity.[1]

In other words, in his doctrine of the basic norm Kelsen failed to distinguish between momentary and non-momentary legal systems. In exercising their primary descriptive function, legal scientists are, as I shall argue,[2] generally only concerned with the former. Accordingly, the formulation given of the 'basic legal science *fiat*' at the beginning of the next chapter refers to enumerated sources rather than to historical constitutions.

6. THE PSYCHOLOGICAL THEORY OF LAW

(A) *Legal rules as rule-ideas*

The abstract nature of the conception of legal rule in the pure-norm sense has been the subject of attack by so-called 'realist' writers during this century. The object of this attack has been to substitute for the abstract entity some actual phenomenon which exists when 'legal rules' are said to exist. In the United States, this 'realist' onslaught has generally seen statements on paper as the only reality underlying the concept *legal rule*. We consider the equation of positive legal rules with 'paper rules' in section eight. For 'realist' writers in Scandinavia on the other hand the reality corresponding to talk of rules can be understood as existing only on the psychological plane: legal rules, like other rules of conduct, are to be equated with 'rule-ideas', in the sense of Theorem (e).

We shall examine the views of two of these Scandinavian theorists: The Swedish writer, Karl Olivecrona, and the Danish writer, Alf Ross. They are especially apt representatives of the

---

[1] Cf. J. M. Finnis: 'Revolutions and Continuity of Law', *O.E.J.*, p. 44.
[2] *Infra*, p. 111.

psychological theory of law for our purposes, since they begin with the same conception of legal rule, but reach totally different conceptions of legal system, namely, those represented by Theorem (f) (Olivecrona) and Theorem (g) (Ross). The reason for this divergence is of great importance. It turns out to be extremely difficult to reconcile the legal-science notion of a unified system of rules with the conception of rule in the sense of rule-idea. Olivecrona recognizes this, and assumes that the notion should accordingly be abandoned. Ross attempts to salvage it, at the cost, as I shall argue, of endangering the values of legality and constitutionality which it exists to serve.

An individual may think of an action as something which 'ought to be done' or 'ought not to be done'; and the fact that he privately ascribes such symbols to the action may show that the idea comes to him with a positive or negative imperative stimulus—in the view of Olivecrona and Ross it typically does.[1] Such an occurrence is termed in this book a 'rule-idea', by Olivecrona an 'independent imperative'[2] and by Ross a 'directive'.[3] It is with such psychological occurrences that they equate the conception of a positive legal rule.

Olivecrona writes:

A rule exists only as the content of a notion in a human being. No notion of this kind is permanently present in the mind of anyone. The imperative appears in the mind only intermittently. Of course the position is not changed by the fact that the imperative words are put down in writing. The written text—in itself only figures on paper—has the function of calling up certain notions in the mind of the reader. That is all.

In reality, the law of a country consists of an immense mass of ideas concerning human behaviour, accumulated during centuries through the contributions of innumerable collaborators. These ideas have been expressed in imperative form by their originators, especially through formal legislation, and are being preserved in the same form in books of law. The ideas are again and again revived in human minds, accompanied by the imperative expression: 'This line of conduct shall be taken' or something else to the same effect.[4]

It is important to notice that Olivecrona is not merely de-

---

[1] *L.F.* (i), p. 46; *L.F.* (ii), pp. 115, 118–20; *O.L.J.*, p. 7; *D.N.*, pp. 34–8.

[2] *L.F.* (i), pp. 42–9; 'The Imperative Element in Law' (1964), 18 Rutgers L.R. 794; *L.F.* (ii), pp. 130–3.

[3] *O.L.J.*, pp. 8–9; *D.N.*, pp. 34–7.   [4] *L.F.* (i), pp. 47–8.

scribing the effect of rules of law in psychological terms, but is equating the concept *legal rule* with an individual psychological phenomenon. 'In reality' the law 'consists' of ideas about human behaviour expressed in imperative form. The rules are the ideas in people's minds. They are not the paper rules, the 'black figures on paper', which cause these ideas.[1] Nor are they rule-situations, externally observable 'patterns of behaviour'.[2]

Rule-ideas are quite different from pure-norm rules. They exist 'intermittently', as Olivecrona says. The rule-idea, for instance, that 'A person guilty of theft shall on conviction on indictment be liable to imprisonment for a term not exceeding ten years', exists at this moment only if someone is thinking those (or equivalent) words. A pure-norm rule 'exists' if it is valid in one or other of the senses of validity discussed in chapter four, none of which involve 'intermittent' existence. The words just quoted from the English Theft Act 1968, *express* a pure-norm rule. A legal rule (in the sense of Theorem (c)) is to be equated with what they mean. The sound of the same words, or the sight of them written down on imposing bits of paper, may *cause* a rule-idea to spring up from time to time in the psychological experience of various individuals. A legal rule (in the sense of Theorem (e)) is to be equated with the result produced by the auditive or visual absorption into the mind of such words.

. It is suggested that the conception of rule-idea is of value to political science as part of its explanation of the constitutional basis of power. It may so be used in performing the fourth of the tasks of general jurisprudence listed in chapter one, that of providing macroscopic information about societies under law. It is an important feature of 'legal systems' in the sense of institutional complexes. Olivecrona offers a psychological explanation of the part played by constitutionality in the effective working of the law, in terms of rule-ideas about formal legislative, judicial, and administrative behaviour, and rightly contends that the greater the hold which such ideas have over the minds of citizens the less will be the need for actual physical coercion by those who seek to exercise power.[3]

If I say that 'Whatever the Queen in Parliament enacts is

---

[1] *L.F.* (ii), p. 111.   [2] *L.F.* (ii), pp. 68–9; cf. *O.L.J.*, pp. 72–4.
[3] *L.F.* (i), pp. 56–7; *L.F.* (ii), pp. 68, 86–9, 101–2.

law' is a rule-idea forming part of the effective role-ideology of judges and other officials in the United Kingdom, I am affirming that the words in quotation marks (or some equivalent) are absorbed during their role-oriented education and that these same words typify internalized assertions, rule-ideas, which from time to time control their behaviour. The quoted words do not refer to a paper rule. In fact they appear nowhere in any hallowed constitutional document; but even if they did, I would not be affirming that judges and other officials are motivated to act in certain ways only when those exact words are brought to their visual or auditory attention. Nor do the quoted words refer to a rule-situation, for I am not saying that, if suitable questionnaires were addressed to these officials, they would justify their actions in terms of this form of words. The suggestion is that the rule is part of their operative psychological make-up, that is, that it motivates what they do, and not merely that it represents justificatory language for what they do.

Olivecrona is unable to erect any coherent conception of 'legal system', in the sense of a system of rules, on the basis of the conception of rule-idea. He equates a legal system with a 'mass',[1] 'conglomerate',[2] 'complex',[3] of rule-ideas. They have a special motivating effect because of the psychological consequences of such key law-words as 'right', 'duty', 'ownership', 'property'; for such nouns—although they have no semantic reference, no counterpart in reality—do, for historical reasons, ring in our ears in a particularly telling way.[4] Thus, the legal system consists of that mass of rule-ideas which owes its psychological effect to the echo of such words in the minds of citizens and officials (Theorem (f)).

But such a conception provides no psychological explanation of the specific value of legality, for it does not enable legal rule-ideas to be distinguished from other rule-ideas. What is the difference in the psychological situation when a citizen (and especially an official) believes that something ought to be done 'because it is the law' rather than 'because it is right'? We cannot answer this question by referring to a mass of internalized expressions which include the words 'right', 'duty' etc., since

---

[1] *L.F.* (i), p. 48.   [2] *L.F.* (ii), p. 76.   [3] *L.F.* (ii), p. 130.

[4] 'Legal Language and Reality', in *Essays in Jurisprudence in Honor of Roscoe Pound* (R. Newman, ed.), 1962, p. 151; *L.F.* (ii), pp. 128, 131, 217–39, 259.

many such phrases are thought of as part of morality rather than law. We will need to distinguish all those rule-ideas associated in the minds of individuals with the word 'law' itself. This brings us back to those categorical assertions about 'legality' which were Kelsen's point of departure in his search for the conception of legal system. The explanation of why people attach the epithet 'law'—in the sense of currently binding law—to some rules rather than others cannot be given without acknowledging that they do in fact think of law in the pure-norm sense, as an abstract field of normative meaning. It seems then that Theorem (f) presupposes Theorem (d).

(B) *Rule-ideas as the subject-matter of legal science*

Whatever its merits as a conception of political science, the straightforward equation of the concept *positive legal rule* with the intermittent convulsions of the psychology of individuals cannot explain the way the concept is used by legal science. When legal scientists say that a legal rule with a certain content 'exists' as part of the present law, or 'is binding', or when they say that, in accordance with positive law, a certain kind of conduct 'ought to be performed', what kind of information are they seeking to convey? Surely they are not informing their audience that, in their society, people experience a certain kind of intermittent motivation, for that would be information which they would be totally unequipped to substantiate.

Olivecrona denies that assertions of this kind convey any information at all: 'Ascribing binding force to a rule means proclaiming that it ought to be followed objectively speaking. This is a value judgment and has the linguistic form of a proposition concerning a property in the rule. But the *oughtness* is no conceivable property.'[1]

It is, however, possible, he believes, for legal science to give information indirectly, when it describes legal rights, duties, or qualities. Such information will be accurate provided we are using words as they are used by the 'common mind' of the community,[2] that is, if we correctly echo the operative mass of rule-ideas. 'It is a question of using legal language in a certain way. The ascription of the right of property to a person is, so to speak, an echo of the rules concerning the right of property.'[3]

[1] *L.F.* (ii), p. 112.   [2] *L.F.* (ii), pp. 3-4.   [3] *L.F.* (ii), p. 259.

It seems then that the most legal textwriters or practitioners can do is accurately to re-echo the crucial law-words which, in the psychological life of a community, are associated with certain courses of conduct. Olivecrona expressly rejects the principle of non-contradiction,[1] and also the principle of exclusion and the notion of a 'closed system' of legal rules.[2] Accordingly, if one seeks to describe the law on a particular topic, this is not to be done by an exhaustive examination of all the rules on that topic which are at present valid according to a determinate list of sources. The accuracy of any description of the law can only be tested by reference to the psychology of individuals.

The analysis represents a complete misconception of the descriptive function of legal science. There are many specialist branches of the law where the normative field of meaning described by textwriters has no counterpart in rule-ideas, because the nature of the legislative material is such that it is unlikely ever to gain a psychological hold over 'the common mind' (for example, schedules of marginal tax-rates). Such specialist law could, consistently with Olivecrona's views, never be described. In any case, the citizen does not require from his lawyer information about fellow citizens' normative internalizations. He wants information about that 'closed system' of rules through which state coercion is filtered down to him.

Ross accepts the conception of rule-idea ('directive') as the 'reality' which is to be substituted for the abstract conception of legal rule in the pure-norm sense.[3] He rejects, however, the equation of 'legal system' with the mass of rule-ideas intermittently revived in the consciousnesses of individuals (Theorem (f)). 'By linking the concept of valid law to the individual legal consciousness, this branch of realism converts law into an individual phenomenon on a par with morality.'[4]

He sets out to reconcile the conception of legal rule in Theorem (e) with the fact that when legal scientists state what is the valid law, they cannot sensibly be interpreted either as conveying information about the psychology of individual citizens or as seeking to influence their behaviour. His solution is that statements about valid law are predictions about the

---

[1] *L.F.* (ii), p. 33.   [2] *L.F.* (ii), pp. 76, 272.   [3] *O.L.J.*, p. 8, n.   [4] *O.L.J.*, p. 72.

psychology of a particular set of individuals, namely, a society's judges and other officials.[1]

He is aware of the danger of circularity, in that the legal system includes rules for identifying the individuals whose behaviour is interpreted. What is provided by the national legal system described by legal science is a 'scheme of interpretation' of the behaviour, not of identified individuals, but of any individuals who are motivated by the ideology of official roledom (which includes the values of legality and constitutionality). The sort of prediction which legal science is able to make is that: anyone who accepts this ideology and these values will, if and only if he has been appointed 'judge' in accordance with constitutional rules defining that office, apply validly legislated directives which are addressed to 'judges'.[2] Such an official will be motivated by rule-ideas about sources ('the doctrine of the sources of law').[3] 'Only on the hypothesis of the allegiance which the judge feels towards the constitution, its institutions and the traditionally recognised sources of law, is it possible to interpret changing judicial reactions as a coherent whole—as regularities constituted by an ideology.'[4]

A further refinement is that the valid rules described by legal science are those which will predictably influence the verbal behaviour of officials. This enables the statements of legal science to be truly 'scientific' because they become subject to empirical test. If the descriptions of the law were interpreted as predictions of rule-ideas which would influence non-verbal behaviour, the mere fact that an official cited a rule would not serve as verification, since the citation might not itself have influenced his decision.[5]

Thus, the momentary legal system described in an essay of legal science consists of all the rule-ideas which (predictably) will influence the verbal behaviour of the officials of the community whose law is described (Theorem (g)). What is affirmed when a rule is said to be part of the law is that it is likely that a rule-idea with this content will spring up in the mind of some official(s) and he (they) will justify some decision(s) by a citation of the legislative material which caused the rule-idea.

Ross's 'scheme of interpretation' (Theorem (g)) differs from

[1] *O.L.J.*, pp. 18, 41.   [2] *O.L.J.*, pp. 34-8.   [3] *O.L.J.*, pp. 75-8.
[4] *D.N.*, p. 88.   [5] *O.L.J.*, pp. 43-4.

the 'field of normative meaning' (Theorem (d)) only in that its ontological status depends on a psychological element. The latter 'exists' as a pure abstraction, as the content of that which ought (ought not) or may be done by law, whereas the former 'exists' as a prediction of the ideas which will motivate official behaviour. The equivalent logical truth-ground to Bentham's unitary sovereign will and Kelsen's basic norm becomes the notion of *acceptability by a rational official*.

It is questionable whether the verification Ross is aiming at is empirically practicable. It might prove too much, in that one might find a judgment articulating much else besides the legislative source-materials which are the business of legal science (e.g. *non-legal* rule-ideas such as 'family life ought to be preserved'). It might prove too little, in that legislative rule-ideas might cause the decision without this fact being revealed in the judgment. In any case, the evidential connection between judicial citations and actual rule-ideas must be a matter of speculation.[1]

But the crucial flaw in his analysis is that it neglects the fact that, pursuant to their role-values, legal officials must themselves act as legal scientists. Ross recognizes that the only 'officials' about whom legal science can convey useful interpretative and predictive information are those who accept (or purport to accept) what I have termed the values of legality and constitutionality. In order that they may apply these values, such officials must *know* the content of the law and *know* that it has been validly enacted before they can make decisions. Such *knowledge* comes to them in the same way as it comes to a textwriter. In other words, they too must ascertain the conclusions of legal science on the topic before them before they can act. They may do this from scratch, like a textwriter, by an examination and reconstruction of all the relevant legislative source-materials—as is the common Anglo-American judicial practice —or they may accept the conclusions of textwriters—as is the common continental judicial practice—or they may accept the unpublished opinions of legal experts—as is commonly done by non-judicial officials everywhere. In whatever way an official informs himself of the valid law on a topic before applying it, what he is informing himself of is not a prediction of what

[1] Cf. *L.V.*, pp. 7–15.

officials will decide: a judge's decision is not a prediction of his own decision.

Thus, Ross's interpretation of the logical status of the conclusions of legal science is one which cannot, logically, be applied to such conclusions when they are reached by officials. His interpretation could, logically, be applied to the conclusions of legal scientists who are not also acting as officials, since the values of legality and constitutionality do not directly apply to them. But even here, Ross's interpretation would not coincide with what legal scientists see themselves as doing: for the conclusions typically reached by textwriters refer to present law, not to predictable psychological events.[1] Ross is right to emphasize that the primary usefulness of legal science depends on its ability to inform the citizen about likely official behaviour, but this usefulness stems from the fact that both are concerned with the same subject-matter, although in different ways. Legal scientists purport to describe, officials to apply, the present law.

Ross's interpretation stems from his dogmatic adherence to traditional logical positivism. For him the conclusions of legal science must, since they are synthetic propositions rather than logico-mathematical tautologies, be empirically testable if they are to be 'meaningful'.[2] Now Kelsen asserted that legal-science statements could be demonstrably true or false. If a textwriter asserts that a rule is part of the law of a community, he can prove that his assertion is correct by pointing to a particular legislative act and to the absence of any repealing or derogating act.[3] But this does not amount to an empirical verification that the content of the rule is the law. Pointing to a source is not the same as conducting a test.

It may often happen that the law on a particular topic is uncertain, and for that reason persons whose interest it is to establish it bring a 'test case' before the courts. Then if two conflicting opinions had been expressed as to what the law was, we may say that one of them is 'proved right' and the other 'proved wrong' by the decision. Strictly speaking, however, what is tested is not different views as to what the law was before the court's decision, but different views as to what the

---

[1] Cf. G. C. Christie: 'The Notion of Validity in Modern Jurisprudence' (1964), 48 Minn. L.R. 1049.

[2] *O.L.J.*, pp. 39–40.   [3] *G.T.*, p. 48; *P.T.L.*, p. 19.

law would be after the court's decision. All that could be said of the law before the decision was that it was uncertain, but that it might be settled (by virtue of judicial determination) in one or other of various ways. Reasons given for thinking one development more legally *appropriate* than another will be reasons belonging to one or other of the models of rationality discussed in chapter five. Reasons given for thinking one development more *likely* than another may belong to any branch of social science whose subject-matter includes decision-making.

The test case represents a legislative enactment, at least in the sense that it provides a new source by reference to which lawyers will justify their assertions about the law. A legal scientist who asserts what the law is now (rather than predicts how it will develop) can never be proved wrong by a future court decision, since it will always be open to him to say that the court wrongly applied the law and thereby changed it. He can only be proved wrong by its being pointed out that the sources which he cites do not yield the conclusion he draws, or that he has overlooked other sources.

Consequently, we can only allow ourselves the luxury of speaking in terms of what the law now is (by means of conclusions whose demonstration depends on citing sources), if we will admit the mental construct of a normative field of meaning, as something about which it is possible sensibly to talk even though such talk must be expressed in non-testable assertions. If one accepts that rational demonstration of the truth (correctness) of a conclusion lies only in empirical verification, then something like Ross's re-interpretation of legal science becomes inevitable and the values of legality and constitutionality can have no rational basis.

7. THE BEHAVIOURAL THEORY OF LAW

(A) *Legal rules as rule-situations*

The behavioural theory of law is one which seeks to show that anything that is said about legal concepts can, without loss of meaning, be translated into statements about observable human behaviour.

Theorems (h) and (i) are based on the writings of Professor

H. L. A. Hart, although, as we shall see, Hart does not consistently maintain the propositions expressed by them in his discussion of legal rules. It will be suggested that Theorem (h)may be employed as a bridging tool between legal science and other social sciences, but that these theorems miss the epistemological bases peculiar to the science of law itself.

According to Hart, the most fruitful way to analyse concepts is to set out the circumstances which typically obtain when a sentence containing the word denoting the concept is used, rather than to provide definitions of the form 'a . . . is a . . .'.[1] In elucidating such concepts as *contract, right, possession, corporation,* and *obligation,* he was able to use (without elucidating) the concepts *legal rule* and *legal system.*[2] He said, for example, that a statement of the form 'X has a right' is true if there exists a legal system containing rules with a certain content.[3] In such an analysis, it is taken for granted that the term to be explicated is a lawyer's term of art, for obviously someone other than a legal scientist could say 'X has a right' in quite different circumstances.

When, however, in his book, *The Concept of Law,* Hart analysed the concepts *rule, legal rule,* and *legal system,* he purported to set out the typical circumstances in which anyone, not just a legal scientist, would use these terms. Accordingly, he had to produce an analysis richer in sociological detail than that required by his analysis of other legal concepts.

Notwithstanding its concern with analysis the book may also be regarded as an essay in descriptive sociology; for the suggestion that inquiries into the meanings of words merely throw light on words is false. Many important distinctions, which are not immediately obvious, between types of social situation or relationships may best be brought to light by an examination of the standard uses of the relevant expressions and of the way in which these depend on a social context, itself often left unstated.[4]

---

[1] 'Definition and Theory in Jurisprudence' (1954), 70 L.Q.R. 37; *C.L.,* pp. 13–17.
[2] 'The Ascription of Responsibility and Rights', in A. G. N. Flew (ed.): *Logic and Language,* 1st Series, 1951, p. 145; 'Definition and Theory in Jurisprudence', op. cit.; 'Legal and Moral Obligation', in A. I. Melden (ed.): *Essays in Legal Philosophy,* 1958, p. 82.
[3] 'Definition and Theory in Jurisprudence', op. cit., p. 49.
[4] *C.L.,* p. vii. Cf. P. M. S. Hacker: 'Hart's Philosophy of Law', *L.M.S.,* p. 1.

In these words, Hart expresses a commitment to the philosophy of 'ordinary language', a style of analysis which makes
the conventional usage of words and phrases the sheet anchor
of philosophical enterprise.

'A term is defined when the sort of situation is described in
which it is to be used.'[1]

'. . . [T]o know what an expression means is to know how it
may or may not be employed . . .'[2]

Two methodological themes emerged from this approach:
(1) All discourse (apart from specialized, symbol-dependent
discourse like that of theoretical mathematics) is reducible to
ordinary language discourse. (2) Ordinary language discourse,
whatever it may purport to be about, is always actually about
physical properties or processes, events and behaviour. These
are the only observable elements in a 'social context'. Analysis
in terms of mental entities is to be eschewed.

It is because of this commitment that Hart, in the opening
chapters of his book, equates the concepts *legal rule* and *legal
system* with special kinds of social situation (Theorems (h) and
(i)). The contexts in which the 'standard expressions' repre-
senting these concepts are used by ordinary men cannot be
classified in any other way, unless we are willing—as ordinary
language philosophers are not—to interpret them in psychological terms. When, later in the book, Hart seeks to elucidate
the specifically legal-science problem of the application of rules
in clear and unclear cases, he refers (as we shall see) not to
'standard' but to 'technical' expressions, that is, expressions
whose significance is discipline-dependent; and at this point he
silently drops the equation of positive legal rules with rule-
situations, and adopts instead the pure-norm interpretation.

If we observe that most members of a social group go to the
cinema once a week, it would be appropriate, Hart argues, to
describe this conduct as constituting a 'habit' rather than as
being required by a 'rule'. If, on the other hand, a regular line
of conduct is accompanied by criticisms on the part of group-
members of those who do not comply with it, by demands for

---

[1] F. Waismann: 'Verifiability', in G. H. R. Parkinson (ed.): *The Theory of
Meaning*, 1968, p. 40.
[2] G. Ryle: 'The Theory of Meaning', in C. A. Mace (ed.): *British Philosophy in
the Mid-Century*, 1957, p. 255.

conformity, and by acknowledgements that indeed that conduct 'ought' to be performed, it would be appropriate to describe that conduct as required by a rule. The line of conduct is the 'external aspect' of the rule, and the criticisms, demands, and acknowledgements its 'internal aspect'.[1]

Thus, to say that a 'rule' exists is to affirm the existence of a social situation—a 'rule-situation', as it is called here—in which conduct is regarded as a standard (Theorem (h)). That the conduct is regarded as a standard means that the conduct is generally observed and that the participants in the social situation express demands, criticisms, and acknowledgements about it.

Rule-situations should be contrasted with rule-ideas. Hart makes it clear that the 'reflective critical attitude' (the 'internal point of view') which exists whenever it is appropriate to describe conduct as required by a rule is not a psychological phenomenon. He rejects the psychological analysis of the conception of rule discussed in the last section.[2] 'There is no contradiction in saying that people accept certain rules but experience no such feelings of compulsion.'[3]

It may well be that if we say that most members of a group 'accept' certain rules, we would not, if asked to justify our assertion, point to the existence of certain psychological conditions, but rather to the occurrence of behavioural patterns and speech acts. But we might withdraw such an assertion if evidence could be adduced to show that the criticisms, demands, and acknowledgements were shams, and that those who made them had no 'feelings of compulsion'. Might we not then say that they *pretended* to accept the rules? Furthermore, the occurrence of behavioural patterns and criticisms might not be sufficient to warrant us saying that a 'rule' had been accepted, for they might be evidence merely of a prudential practice; and such occurrences would be unnecessary to warrant us saying that an individual had accepted a personal rule, for we could say that of someone who ruefully acknowledged his regular failures to comply.[4]

Such questions about the use of expressions like 'acceptance

[1] *C.L.*, pp. 54–6, 86–8, 96, 97–107, 243–4.
[2] 'Scandinavian Realism' (1959), 17 C.L.J. 233, 236 ff.
[3] *C.L.*, p. 56.
[4] Cf. G. J. Warnock: *The Object of Morality*, 1970, ch. 4; J. Raz: *Practical Reason and Norms*, 1975, pp. 49–58.

of rules' have no bearing on the soundness of two contentions which I make in this book. First, both the sociological conception of 'rule-situation' and the psychological conception of 'rule-idea' are of use to the sociology of law. Second, neither is the primary subject-matter of legal science.

Psychological generalizations have their dangers. For example, different kinds of rule-ideas must include different kinds of inhibiting sentiment. 'Moral' sentiments may inhibit in the case of both legal rules and rules of games, given an appropriate upbringing about good citizenship or cheating. 'Security' sentiments may form part of legal rule-ideas—where individuals have been taught to believe that observance of law adds to the safety of their lives—but are less likely to form part of the rule-ideas of games. 'Virtuosity' sentiments (i.e. skill for its own sake) are likely to be more important determinants in the case of games, although something like them may influence the legal scientist who applies some erudite legal rule according to its full logical scope. Such differences are masked in any general analysis of rules which speaks of 'feelings of compulsion'. But generalizations about the speech acts which form the 'internal aspect' of rule-situations have just as great a tendency to mask differences.

In view of his rejection of a psychological analysis of rules, Hart's terminology of 'internal' aspect is misleading.[1] The two sets of circumstances which, he says, must combine before it is appropriate to talk about the existence of a rule both relate to externally observable behaviour. For the external aspect to be met, there must be regularity of conduct; for the internal aspect, there must be criticisms, demands, and acknowledgements. The 'reflective critical attitude'[2] is thus a fifth wheel on a coach; it is a concept redundant to the analysis.

It could be made non-redundant—while still keeping to a psychology-free analysis of rules—if we modified Hart's view as follows: when 'rules' exist there is external conduct, consisting of regularity of behaviour and expressed criticisms, demands, and acknowledgements (the external aspect); there are also criticisms, demands, and acknowledgements which their makers

---

[1] Olivecrona and Ross regard Hart's 'internal aspect' as merely the manifestation of psychological conditions—*L.F.* (ii), p. 265; (1962), 71 Y.L.J. 1185, 1188–9.
[2] *C.L.*, p. 55.

do not express out loud, but soliloquize (the internal aspect). It may be that Hart's description of the internal attitude as 'reflective' refers to such silent speech acts. On the other hand, there would be just as good grounds for saying that, in justifying an assertion that people accept rules, we would not point to the occurrence of such soliloquies as there are for saying that we would not point to psychological conditions.

The proposed modifications of Hart's view would produce a rule-concept midway between rule-situation and rule-idea. But it would not be as serviceable as either of these concepts to legal sociology. If a legal sociologist is concerned to discover whether the 'living law'[1] of a society actually corresponds to the normative propositions expressed in legislative materials, he will be comparing legal rules in the sense of rule-situations with legal rules in the sense of pure norms. He will not be concerned with internalized ideas or soliloquistic speech acts, but merely with what people do and what they say (out loud). On the other hand, if he is engaged on a causal explanation of the 'living law', and in discovering whether it is the normative propositions expressed by the legislature which actually motivate behaviour, he will be concerned to compare pure-norm legal rules with legal rule-ideas. He will not be content with speculations about internal speech acts, but will seek to discover whether the contents of legal rules have become part of the motivating ideology of individuals.

(B) *The union of primary and secondary rules*

What aspects of behaviour make it appropriate to speak of 'legal' rather than non-legal rule-situations? To the anthropologist studying a small, non-literate, tribal society, such a question ought to be of little interest. If the full social dimensions of a rule-situation have been explored, what does it matter whether the honorific title of 'law' is added or not? But to the legal sociologist of the modern state, an answer is vital, since the value of legality is supposed to be a cornerstone of the roles of state officials.

Hart answers this question by distinguishing a special sub-

---

[1] Cf. E. Ehrlich: 'The Sociology of Law' (1922), 36 H.L.R. 130. R. Pound: 'The Scope and Purpose of Sociological Jurisprudence' (1912), 25 H.L.R. 489, 512–16.

class of 'rules of obligation'.[1] The words 'duty' and 'obligation',
he says, are normally only used where 'the general demand for
conformity is insistent and the social pressure brought to bear
upon those who deviate or threaten to deviate is great'.[2] Where
the social pressure includes physical coercion, obligation rules
are 'primary rules' of law.[3] 'Secondary rules' of law, such as
rules of recognition, change and adjudication, are 'parasitic on'
primary rules.[4] In the 'union of primary and secondary rules'
Hart finds the 'key to the science of jurisprudence.'[5] It is 'not
only the heart of a legal system, but a most powerful tool for
the analysis of much that has puzzled both the jurist and the
political theorist.'[6]

Like the Benthamite/Austinian sovereign, the union of primary and secondary rules is a concept intended to serve simultaneously the third and fourth tasks of general jurisprudence
distinguished in the last chapter. It is both a tool of analysis and
a sociological model.

As an 'essay in descriptive sociology' *The Concept of Law* contains the following (intuitively plausible) generalization. In
every society there are primary rules relating to at least three
kinds of subject-matter, namely, violence, theft, and deception;
these are the 'minimum content of natural law'.[7] It also contains
a developmental generalization, concerning the evolution from
a 'pre-legal' to a 'legal' society. In the former, there are only
primary rules, which have the 'defects' of uncertainty, rigidity,
and inefficiency-of-enforcement; the remedy is the introduction
of secondary rules.[8]

If this generalization is empirical, it is falsified by
the anthropological works which Hart himself cites.[9] In none
of the societies which they describe was there a complete
absence of secondary rules; for this category apparently includes
rules of contract, inheritance, and marriage.[10] Furthermore,
Hart's 'defects' were not generally present. They were typically
small, tribal societies in which rules were transmitted by oral

---

[1] *C.L.*, pp. 80–8.   [2] *C.L.*, p. 85.   [3] *C.L.*, p. 84.
[4] *C.L.*, pp. 32–3, 79, 91–5.   [5] *C.L.*, p. 79.   [6] *C.L.*, p. 95.
[7] *C.L.*, pp. 189–95.   [8] *C.L.*, pp. 89–95.
[9] B. Malinowski: *Crime and Custom in Savage Society*; A. S. Diamond: *Primitive Law*;
K. N. Llewellyn and E. A. Hoebel: *The Cheyenne Way*; M. Gluckman: *The Judicial
Process Among the Barotse of Northern Rhodesia*.
[10] *C.L.*, p. 94.

tradition. Consequently, relatively informal modes of rule-recognition and rule-change were all that was needed. It seems more plausible to assume that the introduction of more elaborate 'secondary' rules was due, not to these defects, but to the emergence of literacy and empire. Once rules are reduced to writing, they cannot be changed or developed by informal evolutionary processes. A rule of recognition must identify the authoritative text, and rules of change and adjudication must exist to define those who have power to change the text, and those who have power to interpret it. Similarly, if rules are promulgated from an imperial centre for application throughout an imperial territory, official adjudicators are likely to emerge. It seems likely that these same developments gave rise to the practice of legal science itself.

A third socio-political generalization which Hart makes is an ontological one. It is appropriate to speak of the 'existence' of a legal system where primary rules are generally obeyed and secondary rules accepted as common public standards by officials[1] (Theorem (i)). The significance of these conditions of existence is nowhere made clear. Perhaps they are a heuristic tool serving to distinguish one kind of institutional complex from others. Or perhaps they are diagnostic, indicating that where either condition is not met, generalizable kinds of instability may be expected to appear. Most likely they are simply informative, picking out universal features of developed societies. The complexities of social and economic life to which industrialization gives rise are everywhere the subject-matter of state intervention, and such intervention will use as one of its instruments the regular laying-down and alteration of rules by procedures to which the official role-value of constitutionality attaches. As will appear from our discussion of the rule of recognition, however, this sort of information cannot be appropriately conveyed in terms of secondary rules, if these are conceived of as rule-situations.

As a tool of analysis, the 'union of primary and secondary rules' is used by Hart, first, to analyse 'duty', and then to analyse 'validity' and related concepts.

It is questionable whether particular species of social rules can be identified by the ordinary language approach, that is,

[1] *C.L.*, p. 113.

whether the existence of a type of rule-situation actually coincides with the use of particular words such as 'duty' and
'obligation'. Critics have pointed to the many usages of these
words other than Hart's strong-social-pressure context.[1] However this may be, no analysis based on the usage of these words
in a broad social context will suffice to explicate the concept
legal duty as it is employed in descriptive legal science. A lawyer
may advise that such-and-such conduct is the subject of a legal
duty without committing himself either to the proposition that
some social rule with that content exists, or to a moral-evaluative
judgment about the conduct in question.

As we have seen, the existence of a primary rule entails, in
Hart's view, conduct, coercive pressure, and criticisms, demands,
and acknowledgements. But a rule may be said to exist (or to be
'valid') when these conditions do not obtain, namely, when the
rule conforms to criteria laid down by an existing rule of recognition. These two kinds of existence are possible in the case of
primary rules, but not in the case of the rule of recognition itself.
It can only exist in the former sense, as a rule-situation, consisting of: (1) a practice of recognizing rules as legal only if they fit
certain criteria (the external aspect); and (2) criticisms,
demands, and acknowledgements indicating that this practice
is regarded as a standard (the internal aspect). Just as ought-
language as a whole is used to express the internal point of view
towards rules in general, so validity-language is the appropriate
vehicle for expressing the internal point of view towards the
rule of recognition.[2] It is, Hart believes, senseless to talk about
the rule of recognition itself being 'valid'.

For whereas a subordinate rule of a system may be valid and in
that sense 'exist' even if it is generally disregarded, the rule of recognition exists only as a complex, but normally concordant, practice
of the courts, officials, and private persons in identifying the law by
reference to certain criteria. Its existence is a matter of fact.[3]

It is at this stage in Hart's analysis that the major flaw in his
explication of the concept *legal rule* begins to emerge. If a legal

---

[1] Cf. R. J. Bernstein: 'Professor Hart on Rules of Obligation' (1964), 73 Mind
563; R. E. Hill: 'Legal Validity and Legal Obligation' (1970), 80 Y.L.J. 47;
R. M. Dworkin: *T.R.S.*, pp. 48–58; D. N. MacCormick: *O.E.J.*, pp. 119–26;
P. M. S. Hacker: *O.E.J.*, pp. 160–9; J. C. Smith: *Legal Obligation*, 1976, ch. 2.
[2] *C.L.*, pp. 99, 105.   [3] *C.L.*, p. 107.

rule is to be equated with a rule-situation—that is, with a social situation in which there are two lines of conduct of the kinds described by Hart—what is it that 'exists' or 'is valid' when rule X (which is not generally observed) is yet said to conform to the rule of recognition? In accordance with Kelsen's pure-norm approach, rule X is an abstract piece of normative meaning-content and its validity means that it forms part of a logically consistent field of meaning constituted by it and the other rules of the system. 'Validity' simply denotes system-membership and therefore may be ascribed to any rule of the system, including that rule which specifies the ultimate criteria of recognition.

As to the rule of recognition itself, what could it mean for it to exist as a rule-situation (a 'complex practice')? With a simple practice, like the rule requiring men to take off hats when entering a church, we can easily understand what we should expect to observe in order to confirm that the practice exists: the taking off of hats (the external aspect) and criticisms, demands, and acknowledgements when men fail to take them off (the internal aspect). What should we expect to observe, upon entering courts and official offices, in order to confirm that there exists a rule of recognition? Perhaps the external aspect would consist of the shuffling about of imposing-looking volumes, and the internal aspect of ironical questions like: 'Can you cite any authority for that, Mr. Smith?' At best our observations might lead us to conclude that there existed a rule-situation to be formulated as follows: 'Provisions set out in Queen's printer's copies of statutes ought to be called "law".' Nothing so abstract as 'the Queen in Parliament' can be seen to exist in the behaviour of officials.

Much less could we observe a rule with the complexity necessary to provide criteria of identity for *all* primary rules; for it would have to list all the independent sources of law (such as statute, precedent, and custom) and to indicate the hierarchical relations between them—as does my formulation of the basic legal science *fiat* given in the next chapter. Although Hart uses the sentence 'Whatever the Queen in Parliament enacts is law' as a shorthand formulation of the rule of recognition, it is clear that he intends it to be a complex rule of this kind.[1]

[1] Cf. *L.V.*, pp. 51–6.

If the rule of recognition really is a social practice, then it cannot do the job Hart gives it, namely, that of providing criteria by which all primary rules (statutory and otherwise) can be identified as members of the system. If it does do this job, it must be an abstraction, a pure norm, arrived at inductively from observations of what lawyers do, but not itself witnessable. The formulation of the basic legal science *fiat* is arrived at in this way.

In his discussion of 'rule-scepticism', Hart in fact assumes that legal rules are the entities which the pure-norm theory describes. He says that the view we take of legal rules should not be distorted by the fact that they commonly have an 'open texture'—a penumbral area of doubtful application. They have a 'core of settled meaning' and consequently they are able to provide a clear solution in many cases, even though sometimes it may be debatable whether or not a case falls under them.[1]

What is it that can have a range of clear application and a fringe of uncertainty, if it is not a rule in the pure-norm sense? Doubts about the proper description of rule-situations arise from lack of evidence about conduct, criticisms, demands, and acknowledgements. Uncertainty about legal rules arises when the meaning of words expressing them is unclear. If we asked an anthropologist whether a tribe he had studied had a rule governing a certain matter, he might answer that that was a doubtful case, because of the scanty evidence as to tribal behaviour in such situations, and, similarly, if we asked one versed in English public affairs whether there is a convention governing a certain point, he might say that this was not clear since no situation of the kind had arisen for a long time. In both these contexts, what we are asking about is a rule-situation. But if a judge is asked whether a rule expressed by certain legislative words covers a case, he is not concerned to find out whether people behave in a certain way and, so behaving, make criticisms, demands, and acknowledgements; he is operating with a pure-norm rule. Thus, in the context of adjudication in doubtful cases, Hart's shift from Theorem (h) to Theorem (c) was inevitable.

---

[1] *C.L.*, pp. 121–32. Cf. H. L. A. Hart: 'Theory and Definition in Jurisprudence' (1955), 29 Supp. P.A.S. 239, 258–64; 'Positivism and the Separation of Law and Morals' (1958), 71 H.L.R. 593, 606–15.

Hart's analysis of rules is reasonably satisfactory from the point of view of all the social sciences, except one; and that one is the science of law itself. A sociologist or an anthropologist might well accept that when he said that a certain social group or tribe had a rule of conduct with a certain content, what he meant was that the conduct was generally observed, deviations were met with coercive reactions, and that criticisms, demands, and acknowledgements occurred. But this is not how legal scientists employ the concept *legal rule*. They speak of rules being enacted, annulled, applied, extended by analogy, generalized, inferred, deduced, distinguished, modified, expanded, and analysed. In all these contexts, the primary point of reference (the rule) is the meaning-content of a certain normative expression, formulated by the legislature, by a judge or by the legal scientist himself. When it is said by a legal scientist that one rule contradicts another, it is not being alleged that some people somewhere act in inconsistent ways, or make inconsistent criticisms. The assertion is that, logically or purposively, the normative propositions represented by the two rules cannot stand together.

Hart's attempt to provide a conception of legal system which would simultaneously stand for an institutional complex and for 'the present law', is unsuccessful. For even if both can be described as 'systems of rules', they are not 'rules' in the same sense, nor is their systematization a parallel process. The rules of the latter kind of system are normative propositions, and their systematization rests immediately on the logical principles of legal science, and ultimately on the values of legality and constitutionality. The rules constituting the 'legal system' ('the machinery of justice', 'the law-enforcement agencies'), when described by social sciences other than legal science, are rule-situations or rule-ideas, depending whether the focus of interest of the science in question is 'behavioural' or 'psychological'. Rule-situations and rule-ideas are not systematized according to logical procedures. They are selected from the totality of human life and brought into collections (models) according to any select-and-collect procedure which is thought illuminating. Hart's 'union of primary and secondary rules', in so far as it is presented as a sociological model, is an example. Its principal shortcoming, as we have seen, results from the fact that there

are crucial features of official roles which it is difficult to represent as rule-situations.

8. THE DISPUTES THEORY OF LAW

The characteristic point of departure for American jurisprudence during the twentieth century is that it has been dispute-
centred rather than rule-centred. Sometimes, definitions of 'law'
have been offered in terms of dispute-settling decisions—'Pro-
phecies of what the courts will do in fact';[1] 'what... officials do
about disputes...';[2] '... past decisions (as to past events which
have been judged) and predictions as to future decisions.'[3]

These were not intended, however, as lexical definitions
appropriate to all uses of the term 'law'.[4] They were stipulative
definitions of law as the subject-matter of legal science. For the
main contention of a disputes theory of law is that legal science
ought to be about the decisions of officials.

The pure-norm theory of law adopts the position of the traditional textwriter, that the subject-matter of legal science is the
valid law (a set of rules), the past activity of courts being relevant where it constitutes a source of law, and the future activity
of courts being one of the reasons why setting out the law is
useful. A disputes theory sees the activity of officials, especially
of courts, as the proper, direct subject-matter of legal science.
'The subject-matter of legal science is a certain species of human
behaviour—I mean the distinctive behaviour of those persons
whose official role in human society is to answer, for the community they represent, such questions as arise respecting what
is just.'[5]

In the view of a disputes theory of law, positive legal rules are
simply assertions on paper—'paper rules'. For Jerome Frank,
the most radical advocate of disputes theory, legal rules had
primarily the function of *ex post facto* rationalizations of decisions.[6] Since the heyday of the so called 'American Realist

---

[1] O. W. Holmes: 'The Path of the Law' (1897), 10 H.L.R. 457, 461.

[2] K. N. Llewellyn: *The Bramble Bush*, 2nd edn., 1951, p. 12.

[3] J. J. Frank: *Law and the Modern Mind*, 2nd edn., 1949, p. 295, n. 14.

[4] Both Llewellyn and Frank expressed regret that they framed their theories in
terms of a definition of 'law'—Llewellyn, op. cit., pp. 8–10, Frank, op. cit., p. viii.

[5] C. J. Keyser: 'On the Study of Legal Science' (1928–9), 38 Y.L.J. 413, 416.

[6] Frank, op. cit., pp. 140 ff.

movement' in the early 1930s, however, adherents of disputes theory have increasingly moved away from this sceptical position. Legal rules have been thought of as guiding choices, as well as justifying them (Theorem (j)).

G. Gottlieb may be cited as a recent example:

Any utterance which is designed to function as a rule *must* have the potential of being reduced, expanded, analysed or translated into a standard form such as 'in circumstances x, y is required/permitted'. Any statement which cannot be so restated cannot function as a rule for it will inevitably fail as a tool for guiding the drawing of inferences.[1]

A disputes theory, in contrast to the pure-norm theory, equates rules, not with bits of meaning, but with bits of language. A pure-norm rule may have its source in a book, but it *is* an abstraction, a normative proposition. Whether the formulation of the proposition consists of an exact repetition of a sentence in a book is a contingent matter. The rulehood of a pure-norm rule follows, and does not precede, an intellectual operation, namely, the decision of a legal scientist to systematize it with others of its kind into a field of normative meaning, a totality of what ought (ought not) to be done. You know a pure-norm rule from the company it keeps. When it exists as a rule, it has already left the books.

A paper rule *is* a phrase or a sentence in a book. Its rulehood resides in the *potentiality* of an intellectual operation, namely, its possible use for guiding or justifying choices (Theorem (j)).

The conception of legal system employed by a disputes theory differs in four important respects from the pure-norm conception: first, in so far as it consists of 'rules', they are paper rules and not pure-norm rules; second, it is not exclusively comprised of rules; third, it is a non-momentary system; fourth, the legal-science logical principles of exclusion, subsumption, derogation, and non-contradiction do not apply within it. The 'legal system' is a 'dynamic congeries'[2] of rules, principles, maxims, doctrines, morals, policies, definitions, classifications, and so on, found as part of the tradition of a group of officials. It is a historic (non-momentary) collection of written choice-guidance devices,

---

[1] *L.C.*, p. 40. This is a variation on Ryle's description of 'laws' as 'inference-licences'—G. Ryle: *The Concept of Mind*, 1949, pp. 121–2.

[2] *L.C.*, p. 87.

available to officials for settling disputes. Selection from this amalgam is not dictated by legal-science logic, but is a matter of judgment for the official (Theorem (k)). In the words of Benjamin Cardozo:

I find lying around loose, and ready to be embodied into a judgment according to some process of selection to be practised by a judge, a vast conglomeration of principles and rules and customs and usages and moralities. If these are so established as to justify a prediction with reasonable certainty that they will have the backing of the courts in the event that their authority is challenged, I say that they are law.[1]

There has been recently a great deal of juristic discussion about the differences and resemblances between rules, on the one hand, and non-rule elements such as principles and policies, on the other. This was inspired by Professor R. M. Dworkin's contention that they are logically distinguishable: that, whereas a legal judgment must describe a rule which is admittedly applicable to a case as 'valid' or 'invalid', it may be adjudged of a principle that, although it is applicable to the facts as found, it is 'outweighed' by some competing standard.[2] This logical distinction has been questioned: Might it not be that principles are merely large-scale rules, which cannot be applied with the same accuracy and certainty as ordinary rules, or that principles simply summarize features of many rules, so that a full statement of the rules would make the principles redundant, or that rules, too, 'have weight', rather than applying in an all-or-nothing way?[3]

The answer, I would suggest, is that the logical typing of legal elements is dependent on the typing of systems to which they belong, and that that in turn is dependent on the distinction between the descriptive and non-descriptive activities of legal science. The distinction between rules and principles, to which Dworkin draws attention, derives, not from a difference

---

[1] *Selected Writings*, 1947, p. 18.   [2] *T.R.S.*, pp. 22–8, 71–80.

[3] Gottlieb: *L.C.*, pp. 42, 118–19; G. C. Christie: 'The Model of Principles' (1968), Duke L.J. 649; C. Tapper: 'A Note on Principles' (1971), 34 M.L.R. 628; J. Raz: 'Legal Principles and the Limits of Law' (1972), 81 Y.L.J. 825; Note on 'Understanding the Model of Rules: Towards a Reconciliation of Dworkin and Positivism', ibid. 912; J. M. Eekelaar: *O.E.J.*, pp. 30–4; S. I. Shuman: 'Justification of Judicial Decisions', *E.H.K.*, pp. 723–32; J. C. Smith: *Legal Obligation*, 1976, ch. 9.

in logical type between the sentences expressing them, but from a difference in logical type between the systems of which they are members. Currently valid rules (whether large-scale or small-scale) belong to momentary systems; principles, policies, and other weight-bearing devices belong to non-momentary systems. If legal science is merely describing the present law on a topic, its information can be supplied exclusively in terms of rules, and references to a principle which may have been instrumental in the creation of a rule or exception to a rule will be redundant (unless the principle is expressly incorporated in the rule).[1] But the principle is not redundant to an explanation or justification of the rule-creative decision, and it remains at large, as part of the continuing tradition of the jurisdiction's officials, available to influence the creation of new rules and exceptions to rules in future cases.

In describing the law on a topic as at the time of writing, a legal scientist provides information about legal duties imposed on citizens and officials by legal rules. Some may be vaguely defined, such as 'the duty to take care'; and we may, if we like, distinguish rules imposing such duties from other rules by terming them 'legal principles'. All such rules, however, have the same logical status. They all form part of the same consistent field of normative meaning (Theorem (d)). If the legal scientist makes a mistake (for example, by overlooking a legislative act) he may describe as part of the system a rule which, though formerly a member of a system, is not part of the present system. If there is a debate about whether he has made such a mistake, what is at issue is whether the relevant rule is 'valid'.

The legal scientist may wish to do more than describe the valid law as at the time of writing. He may wish to point out that the 'system' includes various in-built maxims which indicate what the valid law may be like in the future, or which summarize what it has been like in the past. The concept of 'system' here presupposed is that of a non-momentary system. If we say that the Common Law incorporates the principle that 'no one may profit from his own wrong', or the policy of *ex turpi cause non oritur actio*, we are describing principles and policies which, over time, have influenced developments from one momentary system to another in various jurisdictions. If we

[1] *Infra*, p. 97.

describe what English law on a particular topic is now, we may legitimately attempt to set out all the rules to the creation of which such principles and policies have contributed, without describing the principles and policies themselves, because information as to the present law is our target. Information of a different kind, about possible developments in the law, is conveyed by adverting to the principles and policies themselves.

Theorem (k) legal systems—such as the Common Law, Equity, the Jewish, Islamic or Hindu legal systems[1]—are of the greatest importance to legal science. They may be incorporated into the present law of a state, in the sense that, on particular topics, a valid rule merely directs an official to apply the principles of a particular historic system. Even without express incorporation, it may be consonant with the role of officials to have regard to one or more historic systems in developing the law, this consonance being, as I shall argue, the basis of the doctrine model of rationality. They thus have explanatory, predictive, and critical value for legal science.

They must, however, not be confused with 'legal systems' in the sense of Theorem (d), that is, the present (valid) law of a country, nor with 'legal systems' in the popular sense of the term, that is, institutional complexes centring on courts. They are, in the context of modern legal science, comprised of authoritative texts—although in past times when the coterie of practitioners was sufficiently small they may have included a large element of oral tradition.[2] They have only that degree of abstractness which 'this book' has when we speak of two people reading different copies of it as reading 'the same book'.[3]

The borderline of a historic system, the demarcation between those writings which may be used as guides and those which may not, is given by the tradition of a particular group of officials. Hence, what is described as 'the Common Law' may vary from one jurisdiction to another.[4] In the case of a religious legal system, there is, it is true, an unchangeable source of rules and principles in its sacred writings; but these sacred sources are invariably supplemented by authoritative commentaries

[1] Cf. J. J. M. Derrett (ed.): *An Introduction to Legal Systems*, 1968, R. David and J. E. C. Brierley: *Major Legal Systems in the World To-day*, 1968.

[2] Cf. A. W. B. Simpson: 'The Common Law and Legal Theory', *O.E.J.*, p. 77.

[3] *Infra*, p. 130.

[4] *Australian Consolidated Press Limited* v. *Uren* (1969), 1 A.C. 590 P.C.

and interpretative doctrines. Like secular historic legal systems, religious legal systems can only be identified by pointing to the tradition of some institution or institutions.

A disputes theory of law rejects the four principles of the logic of legal science. Paper rules may be used to guide choices in different directions, but they cannot conflict in the way pure-norm rules can. A judge will not be heard to say: 'I must now break "the law" (Theorem (d) sense) since conflicting duties are stipulated by (pure-norm) rules.' Whereas he might well say: 'I have a difficult decision, because "the law" (Theorem (k) sense) contains (paper) rules, one of which could justify deciding one way, and the other justify deciding in an opposite sense.'[1] Bits of language do not collide in the way bits of meaning collide. There is no place therefore for the principles of derogation and non-contradiction in a historic system.

The legal status of paper rules does not depend on subsumption in chains of validity. Paper recognition rules may, in terms, indicate the boundaries of the tradition, but a historic system is not exclusively composed of rules qualified to be parts of the system by reference to rules of recognition. A disputes theory rejects the principles of subsumption and exclusion. It rejects the notion of a 'closed' legal system.[2]

As was argued in the last chapter, there are myriad instances in which the application of law cannot be disputed without contravening legality, instances where there will in consequence be no litigated dispute. Advocates of disputes theory have commonly played down this feature of law and so have been guilty of distortion. On the other hand, they have redressed an omission typical of other theories, by focusing attention on the psychological, behavioural, and rationalistic features of the judicial process.

---

[1] *Infra*, p. 120.   [2] *L.C.*, pp. 87, 166.

III

The Problem of Structure

THE BASIC Legal Science *Fiat*: 'Legal duties exist only if imposed (and not excepted) by rules originating in the following sources: . . . or by rules subsumable under such rules. Provided that any contradiction between rules originating in different sources shall be resolved according to the following ranking amongst the sources: . . . and provided that no other contradiction shall be admitted to exist.'

9. THE PRINCIPLES OF EXCLUSION AND DEROGATION AND THE IDENTIFICATION OF LEGAL SYSTEMS

In the discussion of theories of law in the last chapter, I have sought to show that the pure-norm conception of legal system is central to the understanding of the intellectual processes of legal science. Only in terms of this conception can we understand the logical principles of exclusion, subsumption, derogation, and non-contradiction and the values of legality and constitutionality. In this chapter, I shall try to elucidate further these logical principles and values and to show that the legal system described by legal science is comprised of individual legal rules imposing duties or granting exceptions to duties. I shall also suggest that the logical principles and values of legal science may be encapsulated by the above formulation of a 'basic legal science *fiat*'.

We are confronted here with the problem of the structure of legal systems. Has the law described by legal science an essential structure? If so, in what does the essentiality consist?

The problem of structure subsumes such questions as: Into what units does the legal system break down? What are the structures of these units? Have they all the same structure? In what ways are they identifiable as members of the same system? How is the system as a whole identified?

The disputants to any question of critical morality or politics are not, by the nature of their dispute, committed to the exclusion of any supportive reasoning process. But those arguing about the *present law* in any jurisdiction have already agreed, by the specific focus of their discussion, that many things *are* excluded—the manifesto of a political party in a pluralist society; a religious text in a secular society; the views of a philosopher; a failed bill; the law of a past age or of another jurisdiction; 'my' private opinion.

The legal science *fiat* incorporates the most basic of all the logical principles of legal science—the principle of exclusion. The most important single word in its formulation is the word 'only'. Only rules describing sources listed in the *fiat* (and rules subsumable under them) are parts of the legal system. Only duties imposed by such rules exist. A rule describing one of these sources may be called a 'constitutional source-rule'. Its relation to the basic legal science *fiat* is deductive. A rule 'originates in' a source when it is directly subsumable under a constitutional source-rule describing that source. The listed sources may be called 'independent' sources, in that rules originating in them are not regarded as members of the system merely because they are subsumable under rules originating in other sources.

In the case of any particular system, the first blank is to be filled out by an exhaustive enumeration of the independent sources. In the case of the United Kingdom, these independent sources would be: parliamentary statutes; judicial precedents; and (within very narrow limits) custom,[1] crown prerogative,[2] and resolutions of either house of Parliament.[3] In jurisdictions in which the law-making capacity of legislative bodies is limited, such limitations would also be indicated in the enumeration of sources to be inserted in this first blank. The description of any such source may be cast as a constitutional source-rule of the form: 'Legal duties exist when enacted by a statute of the X legislature (limited to subject-matter Y).' The existence of a

[1] *P.E.L.*, pp. 155–62. [2] *C.A.L.*, pp. 39–44, 592–5. [3] *C.A.L.*, pp. 198–217.

non-legal (customary or moral) standard may be given as a reason for creating a new legal rule, but that does not make the non-legal standard a source of legislation in the same sense in which legislative sources enumerated in the legal science *fiat* are sources of legislation.[1]

The first proviso to the basic legal science *fiat* incorporates the logical principle of derogation. The second blank is to be filled out by a description of the relevant constitutional doctrines which, in any particular system, dictate the ranking amongst the independent sources—for instance, in the case of the United Kingdom legal system, the doctrine that statute law always prevails over case law, and the doctrine that a later parliamentary statute derogates from an earlier one.[2] It would also set out, in the case of Common Law countries, the particular jurisdiction's version of the doctrine of binding precedent—which courts bind which. It would further contain any doctrines according to which courts had a power of review over legislation. These are questions of 'particular jurisprudence' or of 'constitutional law'; although there may be an overlap with general jurisprudential problems—such as, granted that in a certain jurisdiction the decisions of one court bind another, what in general does it mean for the decision of a court to 'bind'? This question subsumes two others, which have been the subject of extensive jurisprudential inquiry: first, can rules of judge-made law ever be unambiguously identified?[3] Second,

---

[1] For discussion of distinguishable senses of 'source of law', see *G.T.*, pp. 131–2, 150–3; *P.T.L.*, pp. 232–3. *C.L.*, pp. 246–7. *P.E.L.*, pp. 146–55.

[2] Whether this doctrine is subject to limitation in the case of an earlier statute which sought to bind successive parliaments only in respect of the 'manner and form' of subsequent legislation is a matter of controversy–*C.A.L.*, pp. 60–3, 66–76; H. W. R. Wade: 'The Basis of Legal Sovereignty' (1955), *C.L.J.*, 172; W. I. Jennings: *The Law and the Constitution*, 5th edn., 1959, ch. 4; R. F. V. Heuston: 'Sovereignty', in A. G. Guest (ed.): *Oxford Essays in Jurisprudence*, 1961, p. 217; P. J. Hanks: 'Redefining the Sovereign: Current Attitudes to Section 4 of the Statute of Westminster' (1968), 42 A.L.J 286; P Fitzgerald: 'The "Paradox" of Parliamentary Sovereignty' (1972), 7 Irish Jurist (n s.) 28; G. Winterton: 'The British Grundnorm: Parliamentary Supremacy Re-examined' (1976), 92 L.Q.R. 591.

[3] A. L. Goodhart: 'Determining the Ratio Decidendi of a Case', in *Essays in Jurisprudence and the Common Law*, 1931, ch. 1; 'The Ratio Decidendi of a Case' (1959), 22 M.L.R. 17; J. L. Montrose: 'Ratio Decidendi and the House of Lords' (1957), 20 M.L.R. 124, 587; J. Stone: 'The Ratio of the Ratio Decidendi' (1959), 22 M.L.R. 597; *Legal System and Lawyers' Reasonings*, 1964, pp. 304–11; E. H. Levi: *An Introduction to Legal Reasoning*, 1949, pp. 1–27; *P.E.L.*, pp. 35–101; *C.U.*, pp. 116–25.

if so, do they bind as statutes bind?[1] These two questions concern the applicability to judge-made law of the values of legality and constitutionality respectively. I shall accept that there are 'binding' judge-made rules in Common Law jurisdictions, in the sense that there are rules having their source in decided cases which some courts are constitutionally bound to apply, and which other courts are constitutionally bound to apply unless some special reason (such as injustice or changed social conditions) can be advanced for altering them.

There is no uniquely correct formulation of such rules, but rather every statement of such a rule is a statement of what I shall call a 'provisional' or a 'generalized' legal rule.[2] Nevertheless, fact-situations frequently occur where the application of the Common Law is clear, whatever formulations of its rules are offered.

By its specification and ranking of sources, legal science identifies the legal system it describes. This closing and ranking of sources are constituent elements of the practice of legal science, and do not depend on positive rules of constitutional law. They are taken for granted by lawyers, in whose training they are usually inculcated without explicit articulation. They must be grasped by anyone seeking to engage in a study of the various institutions connected with the administration of justice.

Two kinds of objection have been raised to the view that legal systems may be identified by reference to a source-listing rule. The first argues that such a view makes it impossible to identify as separate systems those systems which have emerged, without breach in constitutional continuity, from other systems. The second argues that in practice no such list of sources could be drawn up.

The first argument runs as follows. Suppose part of an imperial territory (the whole of which is governed by one legal system) is granted independence by imperial legislation. All the laws which now exist in the newly independent territory cannot be identified as a system if we use the legislative sources contained in the new constitution as criteria of identity, because

---

[1] *P.E.L.*, pp. 19–32, 102–45; R. Sartorius: 'The Doctrine of Precedent and the Problem of Relevance' (1967), 53 Archive fur Rechts und Sozialphilosophie 343; S. I. Shuman: *E.H.K.*, pp. 717–23.

[2] *Infra*, p. 91.

chains of validity leading from individual laws to this constitution would also lead on to the constitution of the imperial
authority.[1] Consequently, according to one view, a system must
be identified, not by reference to sources, but by reference to
authoritative recognition by officials.[2]

Now it is true that official recognition is an important practical reason for identifying distinct systems, but it does not follow
that it is the criterion of identity presupposed by legal science.
To regard it as such, as we saw in the last chapter,[3] is to ignore
the crucial role-value of constitutionality. Officials accept rules
as members of their systems, not because they *choose* to recognize
them, but because they are *bound* to recognize them. The value
of constitutionality directs them to apply rules originating in the
right sources (that is, rules subsumable under particualr constitutional source-rules). It requires them to exclude rules
originating in the wrong sources. If the United Kingdom parliament were to do anything so futile as to repeal the Statute of
Westminster, 1931,[4] and to legislate for one of the dominions,
the supreme court of that dominion would—it may confidently
be predicted—refuse to recognize the legislation. This decision
would, however, be expressed, not by saying: 'This law is not
part of our legal system because we have chosen not to recognize
it'; but by saying: 'We *cannot* recognize this law as part of our
legal system because it originates in a source which is not one of
the sources of our present legal system.'[5] Supposing, however,
that one could not make such a prediction with confidence and
that it was a controversial question whether the dominion legal
systems were distinct legal systems; whatever reasons were
advanced by the disputants, each would express his conclusion
by his own enumeration and ranking of sources. Because the
prediction can be made with confidence, legal science only gives

[1] *C.L.S.*, pp. 105–9; J. M. Finnis: *O.E.J.*, pp. 50–61.

[2] *C.L.S.*, pp. 189–97; 'The Identity of Legal Systems', *E.H.K.*, p. 795.

[3] *Supra*, p. 50.

[4] Section 4 of the Statute of Westminster provides: 'No Act of Parliament of the
United Kingdom passed after the commencement of this Act shall extend, or be
deemed to extend, to a Dominion as part of the law of that Dominion, unless it is
expressly declared in that Act that that Dominion has requested, and consented to,
the enactment thereof.'

[5] On the other hand, it seems that United Kingdom courts would be obliged to
recognize the legislation as part of the United Kingdom legal system—*British Coal
Corporation* v. *The King* (1935), A.C. 500, 520 (Lord Sankey L.C.).

useful information if it decides to regard the new systems as distinct. Such a decision is expressed by saying that, although statutes of the United Kingdom parliament passed before a certain date are independent sources of law within the system (that is, would be enumerated within the first blank of the basic legal science *fiat*), they are hierarchically inferior (within the second blank) to laws subsequently made in accordance with the dominion constitution; and United Kingdom statutes after that date are not sources at all.

The second argument against the view that legal systems may be identified by reference to sources runs as follows. There is often uncertainty, or controversy, about the sources of a legal system or their relative ranking. Accordingly, no line can be drawn, in terms of 'pedigree', between legal and non-legal standards. Consequently, the present law of any jurisdiction cannot be identified by reference to sources.[1]

Now it is true that, where there is genuine disagreement amongst officials and other legal scientists about the existence or ranking of particular constitutional source-rules, the dispute can only be settled by reference to political considerations. But such disagreements are shaped precisely by attempts to apply the principles of exclusion and derogation. Their occurrence is in no way inconsistent with the contention that these principles are part of the intellectual apparatus of legal science.

If there is uncertainty as to whether rules originating in a certain source are ones which officials are constitutionally bound to apply, or as to whether they are bound to apply such rules in priority to rules originating in other sources, no resolution of the uncertainty can be achieved by simply applying the present law. So long as the uncertainty persists, however, descriptions of the present law about topics on which such rules have a bearing must presuppose a resolution of the uncertainty, one way or the other. If a rule originating in the debatable source stipulates duty X relating to topic Y, the legal scientist who is asked for information about the law on topic Y can do one of three things. First, he may include in his description the existence of legal duty X; in that case, he has included the source within the first blank of the *fiat*. Second, he may exclude

---

[1] *T.R.S.*, pp. 58–64; T. Eckhoff and N. K. Sunby: 'The Notion of Basic Norms in Jurisprudence' (1975), Scandinavian Studies in Law 123.

legal duty X, having presupposed the exclusion of the source. Third, he may announce that no description of the topic can, as things are, be offered with any certainty, but that one or other of two descriptions would be correct depending on how the uncertainty as to the source is resolved; he may then go on to advance arguments in favour of prescribing one resolution. In so far as he offers a description, tentatively or with confidence, he presupposes listed and ranked sources. The law he describes, the 'legal system' in the sense of 'the present law', is identified by reference to such sources.

Consider the controversy about 'loss of sovereignty' arising from the accession of the United Kingdom to the European Economic Community.[1] Section 2 of the European Communities Act 1972, makes Community law automatically part of United Kingdom law.[2] At present, it makes no difference to the description of the law on any topic whether Community sources are regarded as independent sources to be inserted in the first blank of the basic legal science *fiat*, or whether Community legal rules are regarded as parts of our law because subsumable under the 1972 act. If, however, there should in the future arise a conflict between a rule originating in a Community source and a rule originating in a parliamentary statute enacted after the 1972 act, the kind of uncertainty we have been discussing would arise. So long as it remained unresolved, descriptions of the law on the topic would have to be offered either on the basis that the Community rule had been derogated from, in which case it would have been presupposed that Community sources were not independent sources; or on the basis that it had not

---

[1] N. M. Hunnings: 'Constitutional Implications of Joining the Common Market' (1968), 6 C.M.L.R. 50; S. A. De Smith: 'The Constitution and the Common Market: a Tentative Appraisal' (1971), 34 M.L.R. 597; *C.A.L.*, pp. 63–6; F. A. Trindade: 'Parliamentary Sovereignty and the Primacy of European Community Law' (1972), 35 M.L.R. 375; Lord Diplock: 'The Common Market and the Common Law' (1972), 6 The Law Teacher 3; G. Winterton: 'The British Grundnorm: Parliamentary Supremacy Re-examined' (1976), 92 L.Q.R. 591, 613–17.

[2] Section 2(1) of the European Communities Act 1972, provides: 'All such rights, powers, liabilities, obligations and restrictions from time to time created or arising by or under the Treaties, and all such remedies and procedures from time to time provided for by or under the Treaties, as in accordance with the Treaties are without further enactment to be given legal effect or used in the United Kingdom shall be recognised and available in law, and be enforced, allowed and followed accordingly . . .'

been derogated from, in which case it would have been pre-supposed that Community sources had been added to the *fiat*'s first blank, and that in the second blank they were hierarchically superior to parliamentary legislation.

No resolution of the uncertainty could be achieved by de-scribing and applying the present law. But it would be possible to prescribe or predict a resolution. Such prescription or pre-diction would involve the following mixture of legal and politi-cal elements. The advocate of a solution might pray in aid that method of resolving legal uncertainty which I describe in chapter five as the 'doctrine model of rationality'. He would point to paper rules and principles (Theorem (j)) to be found in legal texts, such as judicial dicta about parliamentary supremacy, or, to counter these, provisions of the Treaty of Rome. So far as such paper guides were felt to give his argu-ment insufficient weight, he would appeal to political considera-tions. The predictor would refer to constitutional source-rules-ideas (Theorem (e)) which, he might speculate, would be likely to have a psychological hold over the judges, and also to other information he might have about the political leanings of the judges. When we ask whether Parliament has lost sove-reignty, we are asking for a prescription or a prediction of this sort; we are not asking for information about the present law.

Uncertainties in the application of the principles of exclusion and derogation may be tolerable if they relate only to very special areas of life. For instance, within the United Kingdom legal system, in the case of a conflict between rules about privi-lege created by one of the houses of parliament and those created by the courts, it is not clear which should prevail.[1] But such uncertainties could not apply to all areas without making the practice of legal science pointless. If legal scientists regularly asserted that a certain act-situation might or might not be the content of a legal duty, depending on whether or not the source from which a rule originated was one of the sources of the legal system, or was a hierarchically superior source, then the sort of 'law' being described would cease to be of any practical interest. Legal officials would have to choose which sources to recognize and according to what hierarchy, every time they had to con-sider whether a legal duty existed; and the same choice would

---

[1] *C.A.L.*, pp. 213–17.

be needed before they could decide that rules which seemed to indicate that they themselves were officials were truly legal rules. It is because, in modern states, such a choice is usually dictated by the value of constitutionality that legal science adopts the principles of exclusion and derogation.

The basic legal science *fiat* is derived from Kelsen's concept of the basic norm. For reasons which will appear, its formulation differs from his formulations of the basic norm[1] in three ways. First, it refers to enumerated sources rather than to constitutions promulgated at a historical date. Second, although some of his formulations may be interpreted as incorporating the principles of exclusion and subsumption, they do not include (as the *fiat* does) the principles of derogation and noncontradiction. Third, whereas Kelsen's schematic formulations of all legal norms (including the basic norm) are in terms of coercion, the *fiat* speaks of existing legal duties. Nevertheless, the function of the basic legal science *fiat* is the same as that function which Kelsen most often claims for the basic norm, that of making explicit the logical procedures of legal science.[2]

By formulating the basic norm, we do not introduce into the science of law any new method. We merely make explicit what all jurists, mostly unconsciously, assume when they consider positive law as a system of valid norms and not only as a complex of facts . . . That the basic norm really exists in the juristic consciousness is the result of a simple analysis of actual juristic statements. The basic norm is the answer to the question: how—and that means under what conditions —are all these juristic statements concerning legal norms, legal duties, legal rights, and so on, possible?[3]

Kelsen at times expressed misgivings about the adequacy of his characterizations of the basic norm as a 'presupposition' or 'hypothesis'.[4] In an article published in 1966 he stated that 'the presupposition of the basic norm is a typical case of a fiction in the sense of Vaihinger's *Philosophie des Als-Ob*'.[5] Vaihinger sought to distinguish between two senses in which the term

---

[1] *Supra*, p. 42.

[2] The secondary, validity-conferring function of the basic norm is discussed in the next chapter, *infra*, pp. 108, 125.

[3] *G.T.*, pp. 116–17.

[4] Cf. passage translated in *D.N.*, pp. 157–8, and *P.T.L.*, p. 204n.

[5] 'On the Pure Theory of Law' (1966), 1 Israel L.R., p. 6.

'hypothesis' is used.[1] In one sense, he said, it refers to a pre-supposition about reality which is in principle verifiable; in the other sense (which he preferred to designate 'fiction'), it refers to a construct which is 'of service to discursive thought'.[2] Hence, by terming the basic norm a 'fiction' in Vaihinger's sense, Kelsen merely reiterated the view which had always permeated his writings, namely, that this mental construct ('presupposition', 'hypothesis') is needed to explain the logic of legal science.

The basic norm is a creation of theory, in fact of Kelsen himself. It is neither a psychological nor a sociological phenomenon, neither a rule-idea nor a rule-situation. As appeared in our discussion of Hart's 'rule of recognition' in the last chapter,[3] no rule with the complexity necessary to provide criteria of identity for all inferior rules can be seen to exist as part of the social practices of officials. It is highly likely that no such complex rule is ever consciously formulated and applied. Approximate articulations of individual source-rules will be enough to dispose of cases.[4] But this tells nothing against the theory of the basic norm, since it was supposed to be a presupposition of legal science, not a reduplication of verbal internalizations or verbal behaviour. It was invented to highlight the central features of the logic of an important intellectual activity, the practice of descriptive legal science. To make this clear, the version of it given here is termed 'the basic legal science *fiat*'. It is meant to bring to light that self-imposed logical circumscription which legal science brings to bear on the subject-matter it describes. We could dispense with it (or with the basic norm) if we could make the logic of legal science just as explicit without utilizing it. In that sense, it may not be a necessary concept. But if it serves its function well, it is a useful concept.

The basic legal science *fiat* is not a positive legal rule. However, on those occasions on which a legal system is expressly identified, the identification is made by some more or less compendious reference to the sources enumerated and ranked by it. On such occasions, it is not presupposed but expressed (after a fashion). Two such contexts are of special importance. First, the law of Redland may refer to the law of Blackland, requiring it to be enforced in certain circumstances. Redland lawyers may

---

[1] H. Vaihinger: *The Philosophy of 'As If'*, 1924, pp. 85–90.
[2] Op. cit., p. 89.   [3] *Supra*, p. 61.   [4] Cf. *L.V.*, pp. 57–69.

consequently have to identify the present law of Blackland, and that they will do by specifying its sources. Second, there may be a revolutionary crisis in Blackland, and a Blackland lawyer may find it necessary to give alternative descriptions of the law by reference to the pre-revolutionary and the revolutionary systems. To explain the divergence he may identify the two systems, and this will be done in terms of their different sources.

Kelsen expressly refers to the second context as one of 'change in the basic norm',[1] and his views on this question have been used by judges in Pakistan, Uganda, and Rhodesia to justify their recognition of the legality of revolutionary regimes.[2] His basic norm referred to a constitution promulgated on a certain date, or to the norm-creating effect of custom. Such formulations make it possible to speak of a change in the basic norm in the straightforward case of one written constitution (or a customary constitution) containing all the sources recognized by legal science being replaced, at a stroke, by a newly promulgated constitution with new sources. But the change from a legal system identified by one set of sources to one identified by another set may often fail to correspond to this simple model. By virtue of some unconstitutional act, a group of officials may publish a document containing new sources without purporting either to repeal or to revalidate the existing ones, and legal science may begin to interpret the law as a system subsumable under constitutional source-rules referring to both documents (with suitable inter-hierarching adjustments). Alternatively, there may be an undramatic accretion or withering. In such cases, are we to say that the old basic norm has disappeared, or has it been added to?

It seems preferable to formulate the basic legal science *fiat* expressly in terms of sources, so that, by reference to it, any change in the identification of 'the law at present in force' may be made explicit. It will then be appropriate to call it, as Kelsen called the basic norm, the 'constitution in the logical sense of the word'.[3] Changes in the content of the basic legal science *fiat*, as it applies to a particular territory, may be the result of con-

---

[1] *G.T.*, p. 118; *P.T.L.*, pp. 208–11.

[2] I discussed these cases and some of the literature thereon in 'When and Why does the Grundnorm Change?' (1971), 29 C.L.J. 103.

[3] *P.T.L.*, p. 199.

stitutional developments, of unconstitutional legislative acts or of evolution in the practices of officials. Whether we wish to call any particular change in sources a 'revolution' will depend on whether its occurrence coincides with political events of a certain kind. The basic legal science *fiat* itself (as distinct from the content of its two blanks) never changes; or, at least, it will never change so long as legal science continues to be the intellectual practice it is.

10. THE PRINCIPLE OF NON-CONTRADICTION

The second proviso to the basic legal science *fiat* set out at the beginning of this chapter incorporates the legal-science logical principle of non-contradiction.

It may be questioned whether, even granted the universal legal-science practice of arranging legal rules originating in different sources according to some derogating principle, there is also a practice of refusing to recognize conflicts between rules originating in the same source. One of the reasons why the law on a topic may be said to be uncertain is the existence of an apparent contradiction, that is, of provisions which may be interpreted as stipulating both the presence and absence of a duty relating to the same act-situation on the same occasion. This very fact would, however, be a ground for advocating another interpretation of at least one of the provisions. What is assumed in the second proviso is that it is contrary to the general practice of legal scientists to affirm: 'The law unquestionably imposes a duty and an exception to duty relative to X act-situation, so that a legal official would be acting contrary to legality whether he recognized the duty or not.' The legal system which legal science describes is a field of meaning stipulating the totality of legal duties and exceptions to duty, within which no contradiction is allowed.

We saw in the last chapter that Kelsen, throughout most of his writings, accepted the principles of derogation and non-contradiction as part of the logic of legal science. His reason for so doing was epistemological and neo-Kantian:[1] in *knowing* its

---

[1] *G.T.*, p. 436; *P.T.L.*, p. 202. Cf. Lord Lloyd of Hampstead: *Introduction to Jurisprudence*, 3rd edn., 1972, pp. 269–71; W. Ebenstein: 'The Pure Theory of Law: Demythologising Legal Thought', *E.H.K.*, pp. 617, 621–3.

object, legal science *must* know it as a unity.[1] In fact, the principles need no such basis, for their foundation is political not epistemological. Legality is an explicit role-value of officials, especially of judges. One of the ways in which the organized might of the modern state is filtered down to the individual is through official decisions which purport to apply the law. This mechanism would be gravely impaired if judges were regularly to announce that, whatever they did, they would be acting contrary to law. Instead, they purport to 'reconcile' seemingly contradictory legal rules binding on them. Legislatures and litigants alike take it for granted that they will do this. Because legal officials assume non-contradiction, legal scientists who are not legal officials must do the same, since their primary function is to describe the law in order to inform people what officials (consistently with legality and constitutionality) are likely to do.

In an essay published in 1962,[2] Kelsen resiled from his previous opinion that legal science denies conflicts between valid norms.[3] This is one feature of his later preoccupation with the thing-like integrity of norms, to which I referred in the last chapter.[4] Instead of the law as a seamless web of knowledge, the ideal entity becomes the norm, a meta-real 'force,' with a specific ideal existence, which mere cognition cannot split.[5] There is a shift from neo-Kantianism to a kind of Platonism. 'Conflicts between norms remain unsolved unless derogating norms are expressly stipulated or silently presupposed, and . . . the science of law is just as incompetent to solve by interpretation existing conflicts between norms . . . as it is incompetent to issue legal norms.'[6]

My contention is that it is precisely because non-contradiction is a generally assumed principle that legislatures can enact legislation in the following form:

'S. (1) All persons shall be under a duty to do X.'

'S. (2) Notwithstanding section (1), persons of class Y shall not be under a duty to do X.'

---

[1] *Supra*, p. 41.

[2] 'Derogation', in *Essays in Jurisprudence in Honour of Roscoe Pound* (R. Newman, ed.), 1962, p. 339 (reprinted *E.L.M.P.*, p. 261).

[3] Kelsen draws express attention to his change of mind—*E.L.M.P.*, pp. 233, 246, 252.

[4] *Supra*, p. 36.   [5] *E.L.M.P.*, pp. 230, 235, 271.   [6] *E.L.M.P.*, p. 274.

Kelsen's later interpretation of derogation requires the assumption that, in such a case, the legislature silently enacted a third rule:

'S. (3) The rule expressed in section (2) shall derogate from that expressed in section (1).'

He has some qualms (as well he might) with the notion of the tacit enactment of derogating norms,[1] and so is forced to castigate partial repeal of laws as incorrect legal technique. Taking the example of a legislature wishing to change the age of majority for entering into contracts, he suggests that it would be 'correct legal technique' for the legislature expressly to repeal and re-enact all the norms of contract law which have among their conditions the attainment of majority.[2] Consistently with this opinion, the United Kingdom parliament ought to have waited, before passing the Family Law Reform Act 1969 (which reduced the age of majority from 21 to 18), until it was in a position to re-enact in codified form all the laws relating to the imposition of civil liability which include the attainment of majority among their conditions.

It can be seen that the task of legislation would be made much more onerous if the draftsman could not rely on everyone assuming derogation and non-contradiction. These principles make it unnecessary for a legislature to add to a repealing schedule: 'and any other rules which contradict the provisions of this statute'; or to enact: 'nothing in this statute shall be construed as stipulating contradictory courses of conduct.'

If the principle of non-contradiction is presupposed by legislators, by judges and by legal scientists generally, it seems to have the same logical status as anything contained in Kelsen's basic norm. The legal-science practices of assuming determinacy of sources and ranking amongst them, and of assuming that a non-self-contradictory legal solution is always to be looked for, appear to be universal features of the institutions of modern states. If that is so, the principles expressed by such practices have (as was argued in chapter one)[3] all the same claim to be designated part of the 'logic' of legal science.

---

[1] *E.L.M.P.*, p. 237.　　[2] *E.L.M.P.*, pp. 266–9.　　[3] *Supra*, p. 11.

II. THE PRINCIPLE OF SUBSUMPTION—
RULES AS CONSTITUENTS OF SYSTEMS

I have argued that 'the legal system', in the sense of the present law of any jurisdiction, consists of a normative field of meaning, in the sense of Theorem (d), and that it is comprised of normative propositions of a certain kind, namely, positive legal rules in the pure-norms sense (Theorem (c)). Yet not all descriptive propositions of legal science describe positive legal rules. Which do, and which do not, turns on the operation of the legal-science logical principle of subsumption. This principle is incorporated in the formulation of the basic legal science *fiat* set out at the beginning of this chapter. It will be seen that rules are to systems, not as members are to a club, but as slices are to a cake; and that the source-related slices cut by legal science, in accordance with subsumption, include constitutional source-rules, positive legal rules, provisional legal rules, and generalized legal rules.

(A) *Positive legal rules*

I shall contend that legal systems, as the subject-matter of descriptive legal science, are comprised exclusively of duty-imposing and duty-excepting rules. Any such rule contains three structural elements: (1) a positive or negative act-situation (doing or not doing X); (2) an *ought* or *may* deontic operator; (3) the conditions under which the deontic operator applies to the positive or negative act-situation.[1] Whether a proposition with such a structure is a positive legal rule (part of the legal system) depends on whether the legal-science statement expressing it reproduces the product of a legislative source. Only in terms of their sources can positive legal rules be subsumed within the normative field of meaning constituted by a legal system.

Whenever a positive legal rule contains among its conditions, or in its specification of the stipulated act-situation, the enactment of inferior positive legal rules, subsumptive possibilities exist. Rules originating in sources specified in the first blank of the basic legal science *fiat* are subsumable under constitutional source-rules. They may themselves have an implicit structure similar to that of constitutional source-rules, for example: 'Legal

[1] Cf. *N.A.*, pp. 35–55.

duties relating to the parking of motor vehicles exist if imposed by regulations created by a local authority'. Conferring of 'delegated legislative power' by such rules creates further possibilities of subsumption.

Perhaps the commonest device for enabling legal duties to be created from derivative legislative sources—that is, from sources not directly specified in the *fiat*—is the institution of contract. Rules of law originating in independent legislative sources specify the ways in which private citizens may create particular duties binding on themselves, stipulating as an ingredient of the derivative source a real or fictitious consent.[1] This may be illustrated from the following simplified example taken from English Law.

(a) Constitutional source-rule (describing one of the independent sources specified in the first blank of the basic legal science *fiat* as it applies to the United Kingdom)	=	Legal duties exist when enacted by a statute of the Queen in Parliament.
(b) General rules (originating in a statute enacted by the Queen in Parliament)	=	(1) Where a contract of sale of goods (as defined) has been entered into, the seller is under a duty to deliver the goods at the time specified in the contract. (2) Where a seller is in breach of the duty imposed by rule (1) and the buyer elects to bring an action in a court, the judge is under a duty to condemn the seller to pay damages.[2]

[1] Cf. *G.T.*, pp. 140–2; *P.T.L.*, 258–62.
[2] Sale of Goods Act, 1893, Ss. 1 (1), 27, 51 (1).

(c) Particular rule (originating in a contract between Smith and Brown)	=	Smith is under a duty to deliver his pedigree cat (Clio) to Brown by November 30th.
(d) Particular rule (originating in an action by Brown against Smith for failure to comply with the duty imposed by rule (c)).	=	Judge Jones is under a duty to condemn Smith to pay damages.
(e) Particular rule (originating in an order made in the County Court by Judge Jones)	=	Smith is under a duty to pay £50 within 28 days of this order.

In the foregoing example, Rules (b) (1) and (b) (2) are subsumable under rule (a), rule (c) under rule (b) (1), rule (d) under rule (b) (2), and rule (e) under rule (d).

These various subsumptive relations may also be described as 'authorizing' relations. Authority to create legal rules may be conferred by higher legal rules either when a rule-creating choice is required/permitted by the higher rule (as with rule (d)), or when what the higher rule requires/permits is made conditional on such a choice (as with rules (a), (b) (1), and (b) (2)). Theorists have sometimes inferred, as Kelsen did,[1] that rules have a deontic function of 'authorize' distinct from command or permit. This led Kelsen to bizarre conclusions: that an unconstitutional statute (not subjected to judicial annulment) must be regarded as impliedly authorized by the constitution;[2] and that laws enacted inconsistently with treaties must be regarded as authorized by international law, even though their enactment constitutes a delict by international law.[3]

However, although in his major works he explored subsumptive relations through his conception of the 'dynamic' relationship between norms,[4] he apparently came to appreciate that the relations are produced by legal science.

---

[1] *Supra*, p. 40.   [2] *G.T.*, pp. 155–6; *P.T.L.*, pp. 271–6.
[3] *G.T.*, pp. 371–2; *P.T.L.*, pp. 330–1.
[4] *G.T.*, pp. 124–62; *P.T.L.*, pp. 221–78.

. . . [I]n the relationship between a general norm and the corresponding individual norm posited by the law-applying organ, a logical relation exists, insofar as the state-of-affairs established *in concreto* by the court can be subsumed under the state-of-affairs defined *in abstracto* in the general norm.[1]

There is no relation between the higher and lower rules *inherent in the higher rule.* The relation is created by legal science itself, pursuant to its logical principle of subsumption. If a statute permits bye-laws to be created in respect of certain limited subject-matters, and a bye-law is created, it may be said of the bye-law that it is consistent with the statute. Before any bye-law is created, it may be observed that a bye-law with a certain content would be consistent with the statute. The statute cannot itself enact that the future bye-law will be consistent with it.

It may happen that a lawyer is faced with a judicial ruling which, in his opinion, cannot be subsumed under the statute cited by the court as its authority. He may none the less describe the ruling as law, because it is his primary function to describe as law those rules which will be enforced. In that case, he has to affirm a subsumptive relation which he avers ought not to exist. This is one of the instances in which a legal scientist may describe a judicial decision as 'wrong, but binding'—others relate to disagreements about the application of legal models of rationality to unclear cases.[2] Kelsen deals with this problem by postulating that legal science presupposes a norm conferring on courts authority to make any decision they please;[3] and if authority was always conferred by rules, this conclusion would be unavoidable. However, the conception of legal authority encompasses, not merely rule-conferred subsumptive authority of the sort we have been discussing, but also institutional authority. Because of the institutional deference shown to courts, which leads their rulings to be enforced as 'law', descriptive legal science has to insert their unappealable decisions into the corpus of the law by virtue of a forced subsumptive relation, even if, critically, the relation is denied.[4]

[1] *E.L.M.P.*, p. 246.
[2] Cf. H. Gross: 'Jurisprudence' (1968–9), A.S. Am L. 575.
[3] *G.T.*, pp. 153–5; *P.T.L.*, pp. 267–71; *E.L.M.P.*, pp. 240, 244.
[4] Cf. J. W. Harris: 'Kelsen's Concept of Authority' (1977), 36 C.L.J 353.

A similar analysis applies to the case of the unconstitutional statute. If the statute will be enforced (there being no available means of judicial annulment), the legal scientist, if he is to give useful information, must describe it as law. He thereby concedes a (critically inadmissible) subsumptive relation, or he denies that some part of the constitution is any longer law.

Such pathological instances should not distort our conception of system-membership. The normal operation of the value of constitutionality requires the conclusion that if a subsumptive relation is persistently denied between two rules on different levels of generality, then they cannot both be regarded as members of the same system. Kelsen's problem of the treaty-violating legislation does not arise in this context since, as I shall argue in the next chapter, it is not necessary to regard municipal and international law as forming one non-contradictory legal system.

The purpose of subsumption, as a principle for the arrangement of normative propositions within a field of normative meaning, is to enable logical connections to be made between different levels of generality. These connections are not deductive or causal.[1] Nevertheless, the actions of Smith, Brown, and Jones would, typically, have quite different significance for themselves and for others if the subsumptive relations did not exist. If there is consciousness of legal power to make binding contracts or orders, subsumptive relations will reflect social-functional relations between rules. It represents a way of arranging semantic units which is peculiar to legal science and to moral sciences which resemble legal science in that they state the contents of rules created by determinate legislative acts or by custom. The content of an inferior rule is only *given* by the content of a superior rule under which it is subsumed to the extent that the choice which created the inferior rule was among the choices indicated in the superior rule.[2]

(B) *Derivative, extra-systemic, provisional, and generalized legal rules*

Descriptive statements in legal science may not express rules with the three structural elements mentioned at the beginning

---

[1] Cf. *J.D.*, pp. 14–21.
[2] Cf. F. Castberg: *Problems of Legal Philosophy*, 1958, pp. 56–62.

of this section. They may express normative propositions which refer only to parts of such rules. This is a matter to which we recur in the next section. But even if they do express duty-imposing or duty-excepting rules, such rules may not be positive legal rules. They will not be such if the statement expressing them does not reproduce the unambiguous product of a legislative source.

The legal system described by legal science is a normative field of meaning stating what, by law, ought (ought not) or may be done at a particular moment of time (the time when the description is made). It would on any one occasion be practically impossible, as well as pointless, to set out its entire contents.[1] It is, however, practical to relate it to any act-situation, whether the act-situation is a more or less generalized one—killing, killing in self-defence, killing children under the age of twelve months—or a more or less particularized one—X paying Y £50, X paying Y £50 tomorrow. This may be done in one of five ways, each of which concludes with a statement about duty.

First, it may be predicated that the act-situation or its converse—not killing, etc.—is required or permitted by a particular positive legal rule which stipulates the act-situation in question. This will be possible where a segment of legislative source-material exists whose meaning-content—though not necessarily its actual words—exactly corresponds to the meaning-content of the statement about duty. Thus, it may be said of 'using reasonable force to prevent crime' that, in England, it is legally permitted, that there exists, in this respect, a positive legal rule excepting everyone from the general legal duties not to commit violence to the person. One is here merely reproducing the product of the first seventeen words of section 3(1) of the Criminal Law Act 1967: 'A person may use such force as is reasonable in the circumstances in the prevention of crime . . .'

Second, it may be predicated that the act-situation is required/permitted by a positive legal rule, even though no segment of legislative source-material stipulates the act-

---

[1] For this reason, issue must be taken with Raz's contention that: 'The problem of identity is the problem of finding a criterion for determining whether a given set of normative statements is a complete description of a legal system'—*C.L.S.*, p. 187.

situation in question. This will be so when, granted a particular positive legal rule, the statement about duty cannot, consistently with legality, be controverted. The statement then expresses what we may call a 'derivative legal rule'. A derivative legal rule is related to a positive legal rule by a practical deduction.

If a citizen asks a practitioner whether there is any duty not to build a house on a certain plot of land, the practitioner will almost certainly be unable to point to any enactment about that act-situation. But he may be able to assert: 'The statute prohibits all building in defined areas; this plot of land comes within the definition; there is accordingly a legal duty imposed on you not to build.' The normative proposition that there exists a legal duty binding X not to build on Y plot is a derivative legal rule. If it were not a clear case, the practitioner could not affirm or deny the existence of a duty. He could only advance reasons, in accordance with the models of rationality discussed in chapter five, which would justify the creation or the refusal to create a duty. By reference to such reasons, and to any other available information, he might predict the decision of a court or other officer which would retrospectively settle the question.

Third, it may be predicated that the act-situation is permitted, not by a particular positive legal rule, but by the law as a whole (the entire legal system). The negative statement about duty may be said to express an 'extra-systemic legal rule'. An extra-systemic legal rule is not related to a positive legal rule either by subsumption or deduction. It is the conclusion of a practical deduction, in which the major premise is the basic legal science *fiat* (applied to a particular jurisdiction) stating that legal duties only exist if imposed in certain ways, and the minor premise is the statement that no legal duties relating to the act-situation in question have been imposed.

The following reasoning would terminate in the statement of an extra-systemic legal rule:

The only source of law mentioned in the Ruritanian constitution is statute. I find that a Ruritanian statute makes it an offence for 'any commoner' to carry a dagger, that another statute makes it an offence for 'any person' to carry a dagger in the presence of the King, and that there are no other statutes about carrying daggers. I conclude that, by Ruritanian law, there exists no duty for a nobleman not to carry a dagger outside the presence of the King.[1]

Positive legal rules are identifiable as members of a legal system, not by virtue of their contents, but by virtue of the fact that they are subsumable, directly or indirectly, under constitutional source-rules which describe sources to which the value of constitutionality attaches and which are, for that reason, to be specified in the basic legal science *fiat*. Derivative and extra-systemic legal rules have, by virtue of their contents, a direct or indirect deductive relation to the *fiat*. To describe them as 'members of the legal system' would run counter to the ways in which legal officials deal with rules, consistently with the values of legality and constitutionality. If, in the planning law example, the client were to build in defiance of the legal duty, a legal official taking action against him would describe himself as applying the general rule laid down by the legislature. Derivative and extra-systemic legal rules represent important applications of the law, rather than parts of the law.

The fourth and fifth ways in which the law may be related to a particular act-situation, yielding a statement about duty, represent ways in which legal science oversteps the boundaries of pure description, whilst expressing its conclusions in terms of currently valid legal rules.

Fourth, it may be predicated that the act-situation is required/permitted by a positive legal rule originating in a source whose meaning-content cannot be unambiguously identified. The statement of duty thus achieved may be called a 'provisional legal rule'. A provisional legal rule represents one of the possible formulations of a positive legal rule which, though it originates in a source, cannot be identified with any specific segment of legislative source-material. Provisional legal rules are the best legal science can offer when the source in question

---

[1] Such an assertion of the absence of legal duty Kelsen terms a 'negative permission', as distinct from the 'positive permission' provided by a legal norm which permits something that would otherwise be forbidden—*P.T.L.*; pp. 15–17, 40–2. A similar distinction is made by Bentham—*O.L.G.*, pp. 119–20—and by Von Wright—N.A. pp. 85–6. For elaborations of the distinction, see Raz: *Practical Reason and Norms*, 1975, pp. 85–7. Raz's conclusion that 'weak permissions' do not contribute to the practical reasons which guide behaviour cannot be accepted as true of the law, as the example in the text shows.

is either custom or precedent. The legal scientist advancing a particular formulation of a provisional legal rule ought, and often does, accompany the citation of source with arguments (based on the models of rationality) which seek to establish that his is the best formulation.

Fifth, it may be predicated that the act-situation is required/ permitted by an umbrella normative proposition which generalizes the duties and exceptions to duty stipulated in a number of positive legal rules. The statement about duty may then be said to express a 'generalized legal rule'. A generalized legal rule is a formulation which, allegedly, sums up the purpose or effect of a cluster of positive legal rules. That it is the best such formulation can only be supported, again, by reference to one or other of the models of rationality.[1]

Neither provisional nor generalized legal rules are indisputable members of the legal system. They represent important applications both of the law and of the legal models of rationality. The frequency of their occurrence in legal science is one of the grounds sometimes advanced for denying the distinction between description and prescription of law. Yet it is only if this distinction is borne in mind that the specifically prescriptive elements in provisional and generalized legal rules, as contrasted with positive, derivative, or extra-systemic legal rules, can be recognized. It is this recognition which entitles us to demand of anyone making an assertion about duty in terms of either of these types of legal rule that he give, not merely authority, but also reasons.

12.   THE IMPERATIVE STRUCTURE OF LEGAL RULES

The law does not announce, on its face, into what units it can most usefully be split up. There is no *given* structure. We may dip into the well of legislative source-materials with conceptually-shaped buckets of many kinds, and we will then bring up rules, standards, laws of any favoured pattern. One of the tasks of legal theory is to give reasons for preferring one bucket-shape to others.

---

[1] Cf. Hart's elaboration of Kelsen's conception of 'rules of law in a descriptive sense' in 'Kelsen Visited' (1963), 16 U.C.L.A.L.R. 709.

(A) *Duty-imposing and duty-excepting rules*

The answers given in this book to questions about the structure and content of individual legal rules are based on the view that it is the primary function of legal science to give information about existing legal duties. On this assumption, a typical statement in legal science will assert the existence or absence of a particular duty. It follows that the units into which the legal system is primarily to be divided, are legal rules imposing or excepting from duties.

At any one time the law of a country consists of some general rules imposing general duties, and some particular rules imposing particular duties which are subsumable under these general rules. The legal scientist who writes the traditional textbook will usually describe 'the law' by statements about rules whose generality will parallel that of rules (b) (1) and (b) (2) in the sale of goods example given in the last section. The practitioner who describes 'the law' to Smith and Brown will, in addition, make statements about rules on the level of rules (c), (d), and (e).[1]

I take a 'reductionist' view. Whatever the syntactic structure of sentences contained in legislative source-materials, the products of legislation are always reducible to a unique logical form, that of the conditioned imperative or permission. Whatever its surface structure, the law described by legal science has (adopting a metaphor of the transformational grammarian) an imperative 'deep structure'.[2] It is the view advocated by Bentham.[3] 'What is it that every article of law has in common with the rest? It issues commands and by doing so it creates duties . . .'[4]

Bentham was aware that legislation might take the form of 'original permissions', that is, of provisions declaring acts legal which were not previously illegal. This might be done, for instance, to lay a doubt at rest.[5] He maintained, however, that where the state of the law at any one time is described, there is

---

[1] Consequently, we must reject Professor Morineau's contention that the 'individual norm' cannot be used to measure conduct and is therefore illusory— O. Morineau: 'The Individual Norm' (1963), 5 Inter-Am. L.R. 31.

[2] Cf. 'Jurisprudence and the Nature of Language: Contrasting Views of Hart and Chomsky' (1967), 42 Washington L.R. 847.

[3] *O.L.G.*, pp. 177–9, 198–9, 249–50.

[4] *O.L.G.*, p. 294.   [5] *O.L.G.*, pp. 99–100.

no good reason for distinguishing permissory mandates as separate laws unless they are both 'superventitious' and 'alterative', that is, unless they enact exceptions to duties.[1]

Conventionally, duty-excepting rules addressed to officials are referred to as conferring 'powers', 'competences', or 'jurisdictions'. But there would normally be no point in a legislature enacting, for example: 'The police may search premises after obtaining a warrant', or: 'The judge may (in certain circumstances) allocate the assets of a deceased person contrary to the terms of his will', unless there were rules imposing duties not to do these things.

Acceptance of Bentham's reductionism does not commit one to any over-all view of the concept of duty. Bentham himself oscillated between the view that duty was analytically tied to sanction, and the view that it was analytically tied to will.[2] Neither view is entailed by the logical-atomistic function which he ascribed to duty in the context of descriptive legal science.

But such acceptance does run counter to the consensus of recent juristic literature. Critics have rightly pointed out that reductionism of this kind has three notable consequences. First, different parts of legislative material originating in the same source, and different materials originating in different sources, will often have to be read together to yield the content of a single rule. In our sale of goods example, the definition of what constitutes a 'contract of sale of goods' is contained in a different part of the statute from the section imposing the duty to deliver the goods. Second, in practice a particular work of legal science seldom states all the conditions contained in any legal rule. So far as general rules are concerned, this would be almost as impracticable as a complete description of the contents of the legal system. A complete enumeration of all the conditions of the duty imposed by rule (b) (1) in the example would require a description of most of the English law of contract. It would be among the conditions that the parties had capacity, that the contract was not vitiated by illegality, misrepresentation, or mistake, and that it was not frustrated. Thirdly, much of what is described in legal science is only indirectly normative—that

---

[1] *O.L.G.*, p. 169. Ross takes the same view (*D.N.*, p. 122), disagreeing with Von Wright (*N.A.*, pp. 90–2).

[2] Cf. P. M. S. Hacker: 'Sanction Theories of Duty', *O.E.J.*, pp. 131, 135–42.

is, it relates to the conditions which qualify a wide variety of duties, while the duties themselves are not under discussion. Much of property law is concerned with describing and distinguishing various conceptual units (proprietary interests and estates), and with stating the circumstances in which such interests are acquired or lost, whilst the duty-imposing trespassory rules (without which these conceptual units would have no social significance) are unstated.

It is not here contended that legal science should change its units of description. Its information should be supplied in the form most convenient to the topic in hand, so long as it can, on demand, pay up in the coin of legal duty. In Bentham's words:

[Convenience requires that] provisions which are reiterative for the sake of explanation, that is expositive, should be in the abbreviated and assertive form: in considering them we may drop the idea of the imperative form altogether . . . still bearing in mind that in some way or other to some sentence or other of the imperative form they are convertible, and that it is to that convertibility that they are indebted for the capacity of entering into the composition of a legislative code.[1]

There are political logical, and methodological advantages in this species of reductionism.

The values of legality and constitutionality are among the role-values of the officials of modern states. To assert of an official act that it transgresses a duty stipulated by a positive legal rule, or that it transgresses a duty stipulated by a rule originating in a proper constitutional source, is a distinct kind of political criticism. Parts of the law which have nothing to do with duties cannot, in isolation, be the basis of such criticisms.

The logical principles of derogation and non-contradiction cannot be explained if the law is conceived of as composed of logically disparate elements. If it is alleged, for example, that X (the assertion of a power-conferring provision) contradicts or derogates from Y (the assertion of a right-defining provision), the alleger must have in mind at least one instance in which, because of X, someone will be legally required/permitted to do

---

[1] *O.L.G.*, p. 303. In fact, when specifying the proper basis for codification, Bentham writes more often in terms of 'offences' than in terms of 'duties'. An 'offence' is simply the opposite of a duty whose enforcement is to be achieved by motives of the coercive kind—*O.L.G.*, pp. 120–1.

A, whereas, because of Y, there will, in the instance in question, be no such duty or exception from duty. For this to be the case, both X and Y must be conceived of as parts of duty-imposing or duty-excepting rules.

Such reductionism is suitable, methodologically, to legal science in discharging its secondary predictive, critical, and legal-sociological functions. In accordance with one or other of the models of rationality, suggestions are made as to how new general rules will be (ought to be) created, and as to how new particular rules will be (ought to be) created as particular subsumptions under existing general rules (or under posited generalized rules). The formulation of existing rules, and of predicted or recommended rules, in terms of duty is convenient for these purposes, because 'duty' at once indicates the sort of act-situation which the rule tends to produce or prevent.

Much sociology of law will ignore the concept *legal rule* altogether, as involving far too piecemeal an approach. Instead, inquiry will be directed towards roles, institutions, groups, and social classes. One respect, however, in which legal scientists are peculiarly fitted to contribute to the sociology of law relates to their trained acquaintance with legal rules (in the pure-norm sense). Knowing the law, they can (and ought to) inquire whether these rules correspond to rule-situations. (Being untrained in institutional models, role-theory, and other aspects of theoretical sociology, they are not equipped to deal with other aspects of the sociology of law.) The comparison between normative propositions and rule-situations can most conveniently be made if both are expressed in terms of duties. If, for example, legal rules impose conditional duties of repair on landlords, the first step in assessing the effectiveness of such rules is to compare the content of the rule with occasions on which the conditions have been fulfilled and the stipulated acts have, or have not, been performed. The next step carries us beyond mere behavioural correlation, into asking whether the rules were intentionally followed, or at least consciously applied; we are then inquiring into causal connections, by postulating the presence or absence of legal rule-ideas (also conceived in terms of duty) in the psychological lives of individuals. The effectiveness of non-imperative bits of legislative material cannot be assessed in this way. We cannot measure the effectiveness of laws conferring rights or powers if we do not inquire into the performance of duties which are conditional on the exercise of such rights or powers. If, for example, citizens are given a right to vote, the occurrence (or non-occurrence) of acts of voting does not, in itself, tell us whether this law is effective; we need to know whether, when people vote, various contingent duties of counting and recording are carried out.[1]

I now turn to various kinds of objection to this form of reductionism.

(B) *The possibility of reductionism*

It has been argued that reducing the multifarious products of legislation to duty-imposing and duty-excepting rules is logically impossible. Since legislation presupposes a non-factual conception of rights, it is impossible to interpret legislative statements about 'rights', 'ownership', and similar jural terms as descriptions of the factual conditions under which legal duties exist.[2]

All that such an argument establishes is that, in order to describe some legal rules satisfactorily, legal science must presuppose the concept *legal system* in the sense of Theorem (k), as well as in the sense of Theorem (d). A Theorem (c) legal rule may make use of doctrinally-loaded terms, either in defining the conditions of the duty, or in defining the act-situation to which the duty applies. Unless the rule is of a very general character, however, there will be many act-situations to which it clearly does or does not apply, irrespective of the normative import of such terms. On the other hand, there will be act-situations where it will be possible to give more particular information about what is required or permitted only if reference is made to Theorem (j) standards, that is, to the choice-guidance devices which, in the jurisdiction in question, have been framed in the loaded terms.

But if such further information is sought, it will be precisely because we want to know more exactly the conditions under which actions are legally required or permitted. The ultimate point of reference remains the duties which the law imposes. If,

---

[1] Cf. *L.V.*, pp. 30–4.

[2] *L.F.* (i), pp. 91–3; *L.F.* (ii), pp. 166–7, 180–2; A. W. B. Simpson: 'The Analysis of Legal Concepts' (1964), 80 L.Q.R. 535. For contrary views, see A. Ross: 'Tu-Tu' (1957), 70 H.L.R. 812; D. St. L. Kelly: 'Legal Concepts, Logical Functions and Statements of Fact' (1968), 3 Tas. U.L.R. 43.

for instance, legislation is criticized for lack of clarity, this may be done by pointing out that it does not make clear what proprietary interests come within its scope. At bottom, however, if such criticism is to have any bearing on the social consequences of the legislation, it must be capable of being expressed in terms of the legislation's failure to make clear what, in particular circumstances, citizens or officials are required to do.

It is therefore both logically possible and, in some circumstances, essential to reduce legislative material to conditioned imperatives. It is, however, the case that Theorem (c) rules may include points of reference to Theorem (j) choice-guidance devices. In any context in which this reference is material, the information provided by legal science must contain a similar mixture of descriptive and prescriptive elements to that mentioned in the last section in the context of provisional and generalized legal rules.

(C) *The desirability of reductionism*

It has been argued that reducing the surface structure of legislative source-materials to duty-imposing and duty-excepting rules distorts the functions of law, and that we ought to reduce them into individuated units each of which would correspond to a distinguishable legal function.

There are two forms of this argument. Professor H. L. A. Hart has contended that we ought to have regard to the social functions of law, that we ought to distinguish different types of rule according to the different purposes they serve in social life. He distinguishes obligation rules, which tell people what they must do, from 'power-conferring' rules, which tell people how they can realize certain aims, such as rules about the making of valid wills and contracts.[1] 'Such power-conferring rules are thought of, spoken of, and used in social life differently from rules which impose duties, and they are valued for different reasons. What other tests for difference in character could there be?'[2]

Dr. J. Raz, on the other hand, directs us to have regard to the normative functions of law. We should individuate as many different types of law as there are distinguishable legal reasons which might be given for or against any proposed action. 'It is

[1] *C.L.*, pp. 27–8, 31–2, 38–41, 94, 237, 238–9.   [2] *C.L.*, p. 41.

desirable that every act-situation . . . that is guided by a legal system should be the core of a law . . .'[1] He concludes that there are not only different kinds of legal rule comprised in a legal system, but there are also laws which are not rules at all, such as laws instituting rights and legal principles.[2]

Now it is true that very little information about the distinguishable functions of law is conveyed merely by stipulating that legal material is to be reduced to imperative rules. One can go a little further by distinguishing the different types of conditions subject to which duties may be imposed. Kelsen does this, for example, when he points out that, typical among the conditions included in a special class of legal rules—namely, rules of civil law—is the choice of the person for whose sake the rule exists.[3] Nevertheless, the richness of the social consequences of law cannot be captured by such formal distinctions.[4]

However, although the distinguishable social functions of law are not revealed by reducing law to imperative rules, it is suggested that they are not revealed by any other classification of legal rules either. Critics of Hart have demonstrated that his division between duty-imposing and power-conferring rules cannot plausibly be understood to correspond with a simple bifurcation in social function.[5] There simply is no one-for-one correlation between distinguishable functions and distinguishable types of rule. Enabling people to achieve certain aims which, without the law, they could not achieve is, no doubt, an important legal function. But can this be said to be *the* function of, for example, legislation stipulating formalities for will-making? When we speak of the function of a particular piece of legislation, we may mean either the purpose with which it was introduced, or the purpose it can be seen to serve (its social consequences). The former raises a question of social history;

---

[1] *C.L.S.*, p. 144.

[2] *C.L.S.*, pp. 70–92, 115, 140–7, 168–70, 175–83; 'Legal Principles and the Limits of Law' (1972), 81 Y.L.J. 825–9.

[3] *G.T.*, pp. 81–3; *W.J.*, pp. 277–8; *P.T.L.*, pp. 134–8. For further elaboration, see Kelsen: 'Law as a Specific Social Technique' (1941), 9 U.Ch.L.R. 75.

[4] Cf. R. S. Summers: 'The Technique Element in Law', *E.H.K.*, p. 732; 'Naive Instrumentalism and the Law', *L.M.S.*, p. 119.

[5] L. J. Cohen: '*The Concept of Law* by H. L. A. Hart' (1962), 71 Mind 395; L. Kanowicz: 'The Place of Sanctions in Professor Hart's Concept of Law' (1966–7), Duquesne U.L.R. 1; C. Tapper: 'Powers and Secondary Rules of Change', *O.E.J.*, pp. 242, 248–68.

and historical investigation may demonstrate that formal rules about wills were introduced, not to enable people to realize aims, but to prevent disputes arising by stopping people making informal wills, as was the case with the English Statute of Frauds, 1677. The second is a question of sociological inquiry and evaluation. The social consequences of formal rules about wills may be described in many ways: 'They enable people to make secure provisions for those they wish to benefit.' 'They prevent fraud and minimize disputes.' 'They inhibit people from making informal wills.' 'They penalize those social groups who are not accustomed to employ professional assistance'. 'They provide traps for honest laymen.' 'They give work to lawyers.'

An adumbration and classification of the social functions and techniques of the law is a legitimate jurisprudential enterprise. Its social focus must be determined by political evaluations about what counts as important in social life. Its primary legal focus will often be 'the legal system' in the sense of institutional structure, but it may include 'the legal system' in the sense of the present law. The latter need not be conceived of in packets each of which corresponds to one function, but it must not be conceived of in such a way that it becomes impossible to articulate any particular function. (I shall argue that Kelsen's sanction-stipulating structure has this disadvantage, in that one cannot, in terms of the law so conceived, describe the legal function of enunciating standards.) Consequently, the conception of social function limits, but does not dictate, desirable individuation of legal rules. The imperative structure does not itself bring the social functions of law to light, but it does not prevent them being described. The point that one of the law's functions is to support transactions can be made if the law is thought of as conditional duty-rules; for the transactions in question can be included in the conditions, as in our sale of goods example.

The normative functions of the law concern, not its intended or actual effects on social life, but its potentiality of being cited as a reason for action.[1] If conduct is legally required or permitted, that very evaluation can be given as a reason for performance or abstention. The specification of duties is one of the

[1] Cf. Raz: 'On the Functions of Law', *O.E.J.*, p. 278.

normative functions of law. But clearly it is not the only one. If a testator asks why he should make a will in a certain form, he may be told nothing about the duties of executors or of the probate court, but simply that only wills made in that form are legally valid. Thus, it can be said, the law has a normative function of distinguishing valid acts from invalid ones. If, however, the testator asks why it matters whether his will is 'valid' or not, his attention will assuredly be drawn to practical consequences. Guiding action (a normative function) can in theory be distinguished from affecting action (a social function), but in practice they are likely to be mutually enmeshed.

In any case, why should the enumeration of normative functions require any particular individuation of laws? Why is a one-for-one correlation between normative functions and types of law to be stipulated?

The argument for taking this course appears to run as follows. A normative function of the law is discharged when a part of the law is cited as a reason for action. Legal science ought, therefore, in advance of any demand for information, to break down its subject-matter into packages which are convenient for the purpose of giving such reasons.[1]

This would be a daunting enterprise.[2] As it is, legal science conveys information in varying types of packet depending on the branch of law being described: in property law, statements about the circumstances in which titles are acquired, etc., in criminal law, statements about the definition of offences, etc., in contract law, statements about the conditions under which contracts are formed, breached, and dissolved. The legal theorist may be able to discover and make explicit certain organizational features which recur in lawyers' expositions of some of the different branches of law;[3] but this would fall far short of providing a set of intra-branch units in terms of which all legal information could be recast, which is what individuation by reference to normative guidance requires.

The enterprise becomes more daunting, depending on whose action it is supposed the distinguished units will guide. If they

---

[1] Cf. Raz: *C.L.S.*, pp. 140–7; 'Voluntary Obligation and Normative Powers' (1972) *Arist. Soc. Supp.*, vol. xlvi 79, 87–92; A. M. Honoré: 'Real Laws', *L.M.S.*, p. 99.

[2] Cf. *T.R.S.*, pp. 74–6.

[3] Cf. D. N. MacCormick: 'Law as Institutional Fact' (1974), 90 L.Q.R. 102.

include draftsmen, then any phrase in any statute would have to count as one law, since it could be contained in a sentence reading: '(phrase) is the law', which could be given as a reason for a draftsman taking a particular course. It would accordingly be necessary to classify as distinct types of laws each of the different kinds of phrases used in legislation—including linkage phrases (like 'subject to the provisions of this act'), and phrases designed to avoid syntactic ambiguity (like 'or in any such case . . .').

It seems preferable to criticize the way in which legal scientists convey information by reference to the particular contexts in which they do it, rather than to stipulate over-all law-slots for them to use.

The conclusion to be drawn is that breaking down the legal system into units by reference to either social function or normative function serves no useful purpose. It follows that reducing legislative material to duty-imposing and duty-excepting legal rules cannot be faulted merely for failing to do either of these things.

(D) *Duty and coercion*

One of the claims I make for the reduction of legislative source-materials to duty-imposing and duty-excepting rules is that the principles of derogation and non-contradiction apply to them in ways in which they cannot apply between rules of disparate types. The same claim may be made about another sort of reductionism, namely, into rules directing officials to apply coercive sanctions. This is the structure advocated by Kelsen[1] and, with modifications, by Ross.[2] Three advantages have been claimed for viewing law in this way, rather than viewing it as duty-stipulating rules addressed both to citizens and officials.

First, the institutionalization of violence is so universal a characteristic of legal systems that it ought to be incorporated within the definition of individual legal rules. Law exhibits, Kelsen argues, a universal tendency to monopolize violence, that is, to determine exclusively the conditions under which the forcible deprivation of life, liberty, health, or property, ought to

[1] *G.T.*, pp. 20, 45, 61; *W.J.*, pp. 274–5; *P.T.L.*, pp. 33, 62, 119; *S.L.R.*, p. 1131; *E.L.M.P.*, pp. 244–5.
[2] *O.L.J.*, pp. 31, 50–1.

occur.[1] 'If "coercion" in the sense here defined is an essential element of law, then the norms which form a legal order *must* be norms stipulating a coercive act, i.e. a sanction.'[2]

It may be conceded that the institutionalization of violence is one of the social functions of the law of modern states. It may even be the most important function. But if so, the point may be made without stipulating any particular internal structure for rules. There is no 'must' about it.

The second argument advanced for defining legal rules as coercion-stipulating rules is that this provides an internal formal criterion for distinguishing law from morality. If law is viewed as a system of duty-imposing and duty-excepting rules, the content of some legal rules will be indistinguishable from the content of moral rules. Kelsen argues that legal and moral norms are distinguishable, not only by their membership of different types of system, but also because of their internal characteristics. 'According to the pure theory of law the internal characteristic of the legal norm is that it stipulates a coercive act.'[3]

The argument cannot stand alone without circularity. The content of legislative source-materials is often not expressed in terms of coercion, so we are only able to have it in the form in which it is distinguishable from morals if we first reconstruct it into sanction-stipulating rules. Yet it is this reconstruction which is supposed to be justified by its effect in providing a diagnostic, internal differentiation between positive law and positive morality. How can the ability to distinguish law from morality be an advantage flowing from the recommended reconstruction, when the distinction cannot indicate what is 'the law' to be reconstructed? Kelsen's belt-and-braces approach to the distinction between law and morals will not work because the braces have to be attached to the belt.

There is, I suggest, no necessary distinction between the contents of individual legal rules and that of individual moral rules. A positive legal rule is distinguishable from any other kind of normative proposition by its ability to be subsumed under constitutional source-rules which describe sources listed in the basic legal science *fiat*.

Third (and most importantly) it has been argued that, since

[1] *G.T.*, pp. 21–2; *P.T.L.*, pp. 35–6.   [2] *G.T.*, p. 45 (emphasis supplied).
[3] *S.L.R.*, p. 1131.

information about the law is of interest to the citizen only to the extent that it gives him (indirectly) information about the behaviour of officials,[1] only laws addressed to officials are properly the subject-matter of legal science. In so far as a statutory provision does not contain a directive to the courts, it is mere 'ideology'.[2] Most duty-stipulating legislative material will have directive force for courts; but supposing a statute contained a provision which read: 'Every citizen shall be under a duty to do X, but in no circumstances is any official to take this into account in arriving at a judgment or decision'; then, so the argument runs, information about this provision would have precisely the same value for the public as if it had been contained in the manifesto of a political party.

Even in such a case, however, although the provision would have no bearing on the law's coercive function, it would be relevant to its social function of enunciating standards. Conduct of citizens conforming or not conforming to X might be the subject of approval or blame by reference to the value of legality; for although this is primarily an official role-value, its social significance is not limited to the conduct of officials.

Kelsen attempts to cater for the law's standard-enunciating function by defining legal duty as that behaviour the opposite of which is made the condition for coercion.[3] He endeavours to meet the problem that this may include behaviour which is *not* the content of a standard—for example, laws providing for detention of the insane or arrest on suspicion—by defining 'duty', as conduct opposite to 'legally ascertained behaviour' which is the condition for coercion.[4]

---

[1] 'As long as the legal order is on the whole efficacious, there is the greatest probability that the courts will actually decide as—in the view of normative jurisprudence—they should decide' (*W.J.*, p. 270). '. . . [S]tatements concerning valid law at the present time must be understood as referring to hypothetical future decisions under certain conditions: if an action should be brought on which the particular rule of law has bearing . . . the rule will be applied by the courts' (*O.L.J.*, p. 41).

[2] *G.T.*, p. 123; *O.L.J.*, p. 33.

[3] *G.T.*, pp. 54–6, 58–9; *W.J.*, pp. 275–7; *P.T.L.*, pp. 111–17. Consequently, even if a legal norm 'subjectively commands' the application of a sanction, by using a deontic verb of the 'ought' kind, it only imposes a duty or 'objectively commands' if the non-application of the sanction is itself the condition of a norm directing another official to apply a further sanction to the first official—*P.T.L.*, pp. 50–1, 115, 119.

[4] *P.T.L.*, p. 41.

If by 'legally ascertained' Kelsen intends 'found after judicial process', then legal rules could only make behaviour the subject of a duty retrospectively. No one's conduct could be described as being in breach of a legal duty until it had been judicially ascertained. If, on the other hand, 'legally ascertained' means 'legally defined', then there is no one-for-one correlation between the occasions on which the law prescribes or prohibits conduct and the occasions on which it makes defined conduct the condition of coercion. For example, where imposts are levied in the event of goods being imported or land developed, no standard is enunciated by reference to which importing or developing will be criticized.[1] Consequently, the fact that conduct is the condition of coercive measures does not enable us to say whether it is conduct to which the value of legality applies. It is therefore not possible to isolate the law's standard-enunciating social function if we first define the law as sanction-stipulating rules.

The sanction-stipulating structure has political disadvantages. If Kelsen is right in believing that coercion is the law's most important function (and I accept that he is), then legal science will take for granted that the organized might of the community is normally available to enforce the law it describes. It has a special concern with coercion only when it needs to point out that a particular pattern of conduct which the law seeks to regulate is *not* matched by any (or any effective) provision for enforcement. There may be no sanctions provided in the case of many public law duties imposed upon officials, yet it may be predictable that motivation for compliance will be supplied by career-related personal advantages, or reactions of public opinion expressed in terms of the value of legality. Where sanctions are stipulated, there may be empirical grounds for believing that they will not be used. In the case of a proposed new rule, there may be normative grounds for advocating that sanctions should not be used, that the advantage of a standard being observed as the result of fear is not worth the human and economic cost of coercion, compared with the possibility of obtaining compliance by exhortation or reward. Because of the centrality of coercion, such empirical and normative considera-

[1] Cf. Hart: ('Kelsen Visited') (1963), 16 U.C.L.A.L.R. 709, 717–22; A. D. Woozley: 'Legal Duties, Offences and Sanctions' (1968), 77 Mind 461.

tions are of special importance to legal science. Nevertheless, all such comparisons between the law and the likelihood or desirability of its enforcement presuppose that 'the law' can be separately described from 'the enforcement of the law'.

Methodological considerations of legal science also tell against a sanction-stipulating conception of legal rules. Suppose, for example, the law requires farmers to report diseased animals to the ministry, and requires officials to slaughter diseased animals when reported, and also requires the courts to punish farmers who fail to report. If we describe this law in terms of duty-imposing rules, a proper basis for criticism and application of the law would be laid. It could be stated: 'rule (1) farmers are under a duty to report diseased animals to the ministry; rule (2) if diseased animals are reported, ministry officials are under a duty to destroy them; rule (3) if diseased animals are not reported, the courts are under a duty to punish those not reporting them.' So stated, the objects of the law are clear, and criticisms can be made, for instance, if sufficient compensation is not provided, or if the fines imposed are not sufficient to deter farmers from concealing disease. These things are not clear if we formulate the same law in Kelsen/Ross terms, thus: 'rule (1) if farmers report diseased animals, officials shall destroy these animals; rule (2) if farmers fail to report diseased animals, judges shall subject them to fines.'

A similar point may be made in respect of what I have described as the contribution to legal sociology which legal science is peculiarly equipped to make, namely, the comparison between legal rules (in the pure-norm sense) and rule-ideas or rule-situations. If the law is first described only as directives to officials rather than as duty-imposing rules directed to citizens and officials, this contribution would be limited to inquiries about the psychology and the behaviour of officials.

IV

Conceptions of Validity

A positive legal rule may be described as:

Valid/1 = Conforms to a particular higher rule ('is not *ultra vires*', 'is not void').

Valid/2 = Is a consistent part of a legal normative field of meaning ('is a member of a (momentary) legal system', 'is legally binding', 'is the law').

Valid/3 = Corresponds with social reality ('is affective', 'is in force').

Valid/4 = Has an inherent claim to fulfilment ('is good', 'deserves respect', 'is binding', 'ought to be observed (on moral or political grounds)'.

Valid/5 = Is part of a transcendent normative reality.

13. 'VALIDITY' NOT A UNIVOCAL CONCEPT

Theoretical studies about the logical status of assertions made about the content of positive law have often been preoccupied with enigmas of the following kinds. How is it that legal science can attribute validity to positive law without committing itself to value-judgments about the worth of the law described? How can that which 'ought to be' also be something which may or may not deserve allegiance? Is it possible to attribute a trans-cendent quality of 'bindingness' to the contingent products of human acts?[1]

I have suggested that the pure-norm conception of legal system is of central importance to the understanding of legal

---

[1] Cf. A. Ross: *Towards a Realistic Jurisprudence*, 1946, pp. 19–52; R. D. Lumb: 'Natural Law and Legal Positivism' (1958–9), 2 J. of L. Ed. 503.

science. Yet Kelsen, from whose writings this conception is derived, struggled with these enigmas over many years and succeeded in producing only mysteries and contradictions.

In one place Kelsen tells us that an anarchist would not ascribe 'validity' to the positive legal order;[1] and in another, that a communist would deny that the legal order of a capitalist society is 'objectively valid'.[2] On the other hand, he writes: 'Even an anarchist, if he were a professor of law, could describe positive law as a system of valid norms, without having to approve of this law.'[3]

Kelsen commonly equates the 'validity' of norms with their 'binding force', and tells us that the ascription of these interchangeable qualities depends on whether or not we presuppose a basic norm.[4] We have seen that the primary function of the basic norm was to make explicit the presuppositions of norm-systematizing legal science.[5] Kelsen accords to it a secondary function, that of conferring validity (in the sense of bindingness) upon prescriptions.

The significance of this second function has been a source of puzzlement for Kelsen's critics.[6] He illustrates it in at least two ways. First, only by presupposing the basic norm can we distinguish a gangster's order from an order of an official with the same content.[7] Second, the question whether or not there is a duty to obey the law resolves itself, for Kelsen, into the question whether or not we presuppose the basic norm: if we do, every norm has binding force; if we do not, none of them do. The duty to obey is an all-or-nothing issue.[8]

So far as obedience is concerned, the anarchist or communist is catered for: he can refuse to presuppose the basic norm and so deny validity to all the laws. But the liberal critic is put in a

---

[1] *G.T.*, p. 413.   [2] *S.L.R.*, p. 1144.   [3] *P.T.L.*, p. 218 n.

[4] *G.T.*, pp. 30, 39, 116; *P.T.L.*, pp. 30, 50–4, 195, 202, 234.

[5] *Supra*, p. 41.

[6] Cf. M. P. Golding: 'Kelsen and the Concept of "Legal System" ', in R. S. Summers (ed.): *More Essays in Legal Philosophy*, 1971, pp. 69, 80–8; J. W. Harris: 'When and Why Does the Grundnorm Change?' (1971), 29 C.L.J., pp. 103, 106–12; G. Hughes: 'Validity and the Basic Norm', *E.H.K.*, p. 695; J. M. Eekelaar: 'Principles of Revolutionary Legality', *O.E.J.*, pp. 22, 25–9; J. Raz: 'Kelsen's Theory of the Basic Norm' (1974), 19 Am. J. of Jur. 94: 'Kelsen's General Theory of Norms' (1976), 6 Philosophia 495; Nino; 'Some Confusions around Kelsen's Concept of Validity.' (1978) 64 A.R.S. p. 357.

[7] *G.T.*, pp. 31–2; *W.J.*, p. 219; *P.T.L.*, pp. 44–50; *S.L.R.*, p. 1144.

[8] *W.J.*, pp. 257–65.

dilemma: he cannot say that some laws ought to be obeyed and others not (on moral or political grounds). So far as description is concerned, there are problems even for the revolutionary critic. If he wishes to give information about the law in force, he will have to presuppose the basic norm and so ascribe validity to all the laws; he will have to presuppose the basic norm *qua* legal scientist, while not presupposing it *qua* political animal.

All these difficulties stem from Kelsen's commitment to the ontology of norms. Norms, like tables and chairs, either do or do not exist, and validity means existence.[1] Because validity is a unique and indefeasible quality, we cannot distinguish that 'bindingness' which depends on the value of legality alone, from 'bindingness' which depends on other political or moral values.

This is not the only kind of theoretical commitment which entails the conclusion that validity is a unique quality. According to the philosophy of ordinary language, the fact that one word is used is itself a reason for looking for a unique concept. Hart writes: 'We only need the word "valid", and commonly only use it, to answer questions which arise *within* a system of rules where the status of a rule as a member of the system depends on its satisfying certain criteria provided by the rule of recognition'.[2]

He denies, however, that to assert the validity of a rule means *only* that it accords with the rule of recognition. It also manifests acceptance of the rule of recognition; for the use of the term 'valid' is characteristic of the 'internal point of view'.[3]

In what does this manifestation of acceptance consist? Not, Hart says, in any ascription of moral value to the rule of recognition,[4] nor, as we saw in chapter two, in any indication of psychological commitment.[5] But if this is so, why should not an external observer (one who does not share the internal point of view) make use of the word 'valid'? Why should not one who is commenting on the laws of a state other than his own point out

---

[1] *G.T.*, p. 30; *W.J.*, p. 211; *P.T.L.*, p. 10; *E.L.M.P.*, p. 230.
[2] *C.L.*, p. 105.   [3] *C.L.*, p. 100.
[4] *C.L.*, pp. 104-5, 198-9. Hart has subsequently stated that he may have been mistaken when he attempted to draw a distinction between the general acceptance of the rule of recognition and the moral principles which individuals act upon in deciding whether and to what extent they are morally bound to obey the law—Review of Fuller's *The Morality of Law* (1965), 78 H.L.R. 1281, 1294.
[5] *Supra*, p. 55.

that a certain normative proposition is not valid law in that other state because (and only because) it does not accord with that other state's rule of recognition? If he had not assumed a unique concept of validity, Hart might simply have pointed out that either the validity of a law means its accordance with the rule of recognition, or that by calling a law 'valid' we express some moral or political allegiance directly to the rule itself or to the system of rules of which it forms a part.

I contend that validity is not a univocal concept. The fact that one word is used in a variety of contexts does not necessarily indicate that there is one underlying idea, or even a related family of ideas, which comparison of the contexts will help us to unearth. There will, of course, be reasons, which etymology and philology may be able to supply, why the one word has come to be employed in different senses; but it does not follow that significant resemblances between the contexts in which it is now used can be demonstrated by positing an underlying meaning. The original sense of 'valid' is probably that of 'strength';[1] but that etymological fact can tell us nothing of interest about the enigmas mentioned at the beginning of this section.

These enigmas and the problems about validity arising out of major theories like those of Kelsen and Hart can only be dissipated by recognizing that, whatever its origin, there are now several conceptions of validity in use. There are set out at the beginning of this chapter five different senses in which the adjective 'valid' has sometimes been applied to positive legal rules. Legal systems can also be described as valid in all these senses, save that, strictly speaking, only a sub-system can be valid/2.

The third and fourth senses differ from the others in two respects. First, they are relative qualities: a rule may be more or less effective, and the allegiance which it deserves may be subject to being outweighed (more or less easily) by particular political or moral considerations. Second, Validity/3 and 4 are cluster conceptions. A range of notions is comprised within that 'social reality', by reference to which a rule may be said to be effective; and a range of moral, political, and prudential considerations may provide the background for ascriptions of

---

[1] *L.V.*, pp. 37–42.

worthiness. Validity/1, 2, and 5 are, in contrast, absolute and unitary conceptions.

Ascription of the relevant quality to a rule may be made without using the word 'valid' at all. No contention is here made about the proper employment of words. It may be that the English word 'valid' is commonly used in some of these contexts and only rarely in others; or that usages of the dictionary equivalent of 'valid' in other languages differ markedly from its usage in English. Given diversities caused by culture, class, age, and region, it is probably chimerical to look for consistency in the usage of such words even within one linguistic group.

What matters are the contextual differences, to the extent that they exemplify features of legal science and of other social appraisals of law. I shall consider, from this point of view, the usefulness, or otherwise, of these diverging predicative qualities of legal rules. I shall seek to show the centrality of the first two conceptions of validity to descriptive legal science and to show that these predicates apply most appropriately to rules in the pure-norm sense.

14. MOMENTARY AND NON-MOMENTARY LEGAL SYSTEMS

Before we can distinguish the different conceptions of validity, we must make more explicit the two conceptions of system employed by legal science in discharging its descriptive, predictive, and critical functions. We must distinguish 'the legal system', in the sense of the present law, from 'the legal system', in the sense of the historic congeries of written choice-guidance devices forming part of the tradition of some body of officials.[1]

In exercising their primary descriptive function, legal scientists are generally only concerned with momentary legal systems. A momentary legal system consists of all the mutually consistent legal rules governing an area of human conduct—usually within a territory—which is at a particular moment in time required, prohibited, or permitted by law. An essay in legal science presupposes the existence of such a system. Legal scientists may often presuppose the existence of different momentary legal systems existing at different times in the

[1] *Supra*, p. 68.

history of a community. For instance, if it is said that a rule with a certain content was valid law in the past, but is not so today, what is meant is that, at any one of a range of past occasions, a full statement of the law on a particular topic would have included the rule, but that is not so at the moment of writing.

If a question is asked of the form: 'What was the law in England (on a certain topic) during the seventeenth century?' the appropriate answer may always include assertions that it differed at different times during the century. This is true whatever period is specified in such a question. In principle, then, the law—that is, the field of meaning which is the subject-matter of descriptive legal science—is what it is only at a particular moment in time.

Cautious writers of legal textbooks always state in their prefaces that the law described is that in force on a certain date. If a textwriter sets out the law as at 1 January 1960, and legislation comes into force on 1 January 1970, altering the law he described, his book becomes out of date; but it would be wholly inappropriate to say that he had made a mistake in his description of the law, that he had 'got the law wrong'.

This is not changed by the fact that the law in force in 1970 includes legislation with retrospective effect back to 1960. The correct description of the situation is that the law in force in 1970 includes a rule that X should have been done in 1960; but that the law in force in 1960 did not require X to be done in 1960. There is nothing at all inconsistent between the conception of a momentary legal system and the occasional practice of legislating retrospectively. Legal science describes duties and exceptions stipulated by rules which are now valid (valid/2), and the act-situations to which these duties and exceptions relate have whatever temporal dimensions the legislature chooses to give them. It is, of course, true that if retrospective legislation were commonly resorted to, descriptive legal science would become pointless. One could not rely on information about one's legal duties if it were extremely likely that, whenever it became relevant to official decisions, what had been one's duty had been retrospectively changed.[1]

It was the structure of such momentary legal systems that we investigated in the last chapter. We saw that the statement of

[1] Cf. L. L. Fuller: *The Morality of Law*, 2nd edn., 1969, pp. 39, 42, 210–12.

rules comprised in such systems might often include references to normative standards which could not be reduced to the factual conditions under which legal duties exist.[1] These standards, presupposed in the articulation of legal rules, are themselves parts of one or more historic, non-momentary legal systems.[2] Legal scientists who give information about them are not simply engaging in subjective legal politics. It is this feature of legal science which is the principal omission from Kelsen's pure theory of law.

Kelsen asserted that his legal norm-structure, by requiring law to be cast in the canonical form of conditioned stipulations about sanctions, provided a logical tool for distinguishing legislative material which is 'legally relevant' from that which is merely 'ideological'. For instance, he says, if the legislature were to enact a 'solemn recognition of the merits of a statesman', the content of the enactment would not be legally relevant since it would not set out conditions for the application of sanctions.[3]

It is true that such 'ideological' contents of statutes would not be legally relevant in the same way that legislative material is ordinarily legally relevant. A recital of what the legislature had enacted would not enter into a mere description of the currently valid/2 laws. It might, however, be legally relevant in another way: it might function as a choice-guidance device which would influence officials in future developments of the law. If this seemed likely, a recital of what the legislature had enacted would be relevant to predictions about how new individual legal rules were likely to be created in hypothetical situations, and it would be relevant as providing an argument (within the doctrine model of rationality) for justifying such developments. The ideological provision would be a paper standard forming part of a non-momentary legal system, if there were good empirical grounds for believing that it would influence the change from one momentary legal system to another.

Supposing the legislature enacted:

S.(1) Comrade Napoleon is always right.
S.(2) Anyone who publicly denies that Comrade Napoleon is always right commits the offence of high treason.
S.(3) Anyone guilty of the offence of high treason shall be shot.

---

[1] *Supra*, p. 97.   [2] *Supra*, p. 68.   [3] *G.T.*, p. 123.

In describing the present law, legal science need not recite the legislative material contained in section (1). Adopting Kelsen's structure, the law may be described: 'Officials ought to sentence to be shot those who publicly deny that Comrade Napoleon is always right.' Adopting the structure advocated in the last chapter, the law may be described: 'Citizens are under a duty not to deny publicly that Comrade Napoleon is always right. Officials are under a duty to sentence to be shot anyone who does deny it.'

But mere description is not all that legal science ought to offer, by way of providing useful information to those unacquainted with the law. It ought to add (citing section (1)) that the infallibility of Comrade Napoleon is part of the ideology of the state, and that questioning it is regarded as such a threat to society as to be described with the evocative expression 'high treason'. This being so, officials who may confidently be assumed to share and to wish to strengthen the ideology of the state, are likely to give a wide construction to the word 'publicly' in doubtful cases.

Ideological provisions, with a status equivalent to that of section (1) of the Comrade Napoleon statute, abound in legislative source-materials. They may be of many kinds: religious, socialist, racialist, individualist. If they predictably will go on influencing officials' legal decisions, they constitute parts of continuing legal systems. In parliamentary democracies, ideological provisions which have in recent years received most attention are those according 'rights'.

There are at least four conceptions of 'rights' which can be expounded, non-ideologically, in terms of currently valid, duty-imposing legal rules. First, X may be said to have a right to do A (a 'mere liberty'), simply because the law is silent about A. This is equivalent to the assertion of an extra-systemic duty-excepting legal rule about A.[1] Second, X may be said to have a right to do A (a 'bare privilege'), where what is reported is the existence of a valid/2, positive, duty-excepting legal rule. Third, X may be said to have a right to do A (an 'interest-right'), where what is reported is the existence of a positive rule or rules imposing a duty or duties not to interfere with X's doing A. Fourth, X may be said to have a right (a 'claim-

---

[1] *Supra*, p. 90.

right'), where what is reported is the existence of a positive legal rule imposing a duty on Y to do B if X chooses that B should be done.[1] The relative usefulness of these conceptions turns on considerations related to the context in which legal information is supplied.[2]

But the significance of assertions about 'rights' appearing in constitutions or other hallowed documents cannot be so reduced to statements about duties. Once we have set out all the law on a topic, the fact that such a provision is part of a legal tradition, part of a historic, non-momentary legal system, has to be added, for it may be cited as a reason for creating new (particular or general) legal rules in actual or hypothetical instances where the present law is not clear. Its total possible impact cannot be spelt out in terms of provisional legal rules,[3] for we cannot envisage all the situations where its citation may be thought appropriate. Its operation is at large.

15. VALIDITY AND SYSTEM-MEMBERSHIP

(A) *Validity within momentary systems*

As we saw in the last chapter, the legal-science logical principles of exclusion, subsumption, derogation, and non-contradiction are employed in constructing momentary legal systems. Their deployment involves the first two conceptions of validity cited at the beginning of this chapter. I shall now seek to show that, of the theorems set out at the beginning of chapter two, theorem (d)—the pure-norm conception—is the one which best captures the idea of a momentary system.

Valid/1 is the commonest sense in which the term is used in the day-to-day administration of the law. Usually when the 'validity' of, say a bye-law or ministerial regulation is challenged, it is on the grounds that it does not conform to some particular authorizing statute. Validity/1 is thus a relational conception. It relates two rules of law.

Such a relational conception makes sense if we adopt the pure-norm conception of rules (as normative propositions). If a

---

[1] Cf. *P.T.L.*, pp. 15–17, 40–2, 138; N.A., pp. 85–6, 88–90.
[2] Cf. Hart: 'Bentham on Legal Rights', *O.E.J.*, p. 171; MacCormick: 'Rights in Legislation', *L.M.S.*, p. 189.
[3] *Supra*, p. 91.

statute provides: 'The minister may issue regulations governing the sale of food for human consumption and may impose a fine not exceeding £50 for any breach of such regulations'; and the minister issues a regulation which reads: 'It shall be an offence punishable by a fine of not more than £50 to sell pet-food during the hours of darkness'; the minister's regulation will be invalid because what is meant cannot be logically subsumed under the meaning of that which the legislature enacted.

The word 'valid' is used in the sense of valid/2 comparatively seldom. It is so used when it is said, for example: 'These two contradictory statutory provisions cannot both be valid.' Usually, that valid/2 is true of a positive legal rule is implicitly asserted, by some such statement as: 'Under our law, citizens are under a duty to do X in circumstances Y.' Such a statement may logically be challenged by showing that the rule affirmed to be part of the law is not consistent with any other part of the law. It may be challenged, for example, by showing that there is no chain of validity/1 stretching between it and some constitutional source-rule—that although it is valid/1 relative to a particular higher rule, that rule itself is not valid/1 relative to a yet higher rule. Alternatively, the validity/2 of the rule might be challenged on the grounds that a later rule with a similar chain of validity/1 had been enacted which derogated from the challenged rule; or that there was a contradictory rule with a chain of validity/1 stretching to a superior constitutional source-rule.

To be valid/2, a positive legal rule must be consistent with the rest of the system of which it is supposed to form a part. This conception, too, makes sense if 'system' is equated with a non-contradictory field of normative meaning (Theorem (d)). Whether a Theorem (c) rule is part of a Theorem (d) system depends, in principle, on an application of all four of the legal-science principles of logical arrangement. The rule must be related, in accordance with the principle of subsumption, to an independent source-rule. The independent source must be one of the list of sources by reference to which, in accordance with the principle of exclusion, the system is identified. In accordance with the principle of derogation, the rule in question must not be inconsistent with a later or superior rule. And in accordance with the principle of non-contradiction, it must not be inconsistent with a rule of equivalent status. Validity/2 is the predicative complement of the basic *fiat* of legal science which, as we saw in the last chapter, encapsulates these four principles.

Could the rule-predicates, which I have distinguished as the first two conceptions of validity, be explained in terms of any of the other conceptions of 'system' discussed in chapter two? Can there be system-membership without Theorem (d)?

The only possible candidates are Theorem (b)—the sovereign-will conception—and Theorem (g)—the prediction-of-official behaviour conception. Theorem (k) legal systems are historic collections, and so not momentary systems at all.[1] Hart's conception of a legal system as a complex social situation (Theorem (i)) might be presupposed by a 'descriptive sociology',[2] but cannot be that conception of system presupposed by descriptive legal science when the four legal-science logical principles are deployed and contradictions denied. Hence (as we saw), when he came to analyse 'validity', Hart abandoned the equation of 'rule' with rule-situation.[3] Nor can the first two conceptions of validity be explained in terms of Theorem (f); there can be no logical relations between the mass of rule-ideas intermittently revived in the minds of members of a political community. It is consequently not surprising that Olivecrona regarded assertions about binding (valid/2) laws as devoid of meaning.[4]

Theorems (b) and (g) purport to provide bases for the logic of legal science and for the conceptions of validity/1 and validity/2. We saw that Bentham's and Ross's alternatives to Kelsen's basic norm were, respectively, the 'logic of the will',[5] and 'acceptability by a rational official'.[6]

Supposing a legal scientist constructs the following piece of reasoning.

I find that a Ruritanian statute makes it an offence to sell drugs X, Y, and Z, that another statute makes it an offence to sell any drugs on Sundays; that the only source of Ruritanian law is statute; and that there are no other statutes about selling drugs. I conclude that there is no rule of Ruritanian law prohibiting the sale of drugs, other than X, Y, and Z, on any day from Monday to Saturday.

---

[1] *Supra*, p. 68. [2] *Supra*, p. 53.
[3] *Supra*, p. 60. Hart assumed that the only conception of validity used in legal discourse was validity/1 and hence was unable to understand how Kelsen's basic norm could be described as 'valid' (*C.L.*, p. 106). It is, of course, valid/2.
[4] *Supra*, p. 47. [5] *Supra*, p. 33. [6] *Supra*, p. 48.

Such reasoning applies the principle of exclusion, and pre-supposes the basic legal science *fiat*—it assumes that legal duties can exist only if imposed by rules originating in determinate sources. It deals with laws and the legal system as normative propositions (Theorems (c) and (d)).

We could rephrase the reasoning consistently with Theorems (a) and (b) as follows:

The law says you mustn't sell drugs X, Y, and Z, and that you mustn't sell any drugs on Sundays, and nothing else about selling drugs; so it must allow you to sell other drugs from Monday to Saturday, since it would be irrational of the law to make those two particular prohibitions if it intended any more general prohibition.

Consonant with Theorems (e) and (g), the reasoning would run:

Persons who exercise official roles in Ruritania are commonly moti-vated by the following rule-idea: 'we ought to call rules "legal" when, and only when, they are created by statutes of the legislature.' This being so, it is likely that, if anyone were prosecuted for selling drugs, they would only accept rule-ideas with the following contents to be found in statutes: 'selling drugs X, Y, and Z is an offence'; 'selling any drugs on Sundays is an offence'. Assuming the officials of Ruritania to be rational men, it is therefore extremely unlikely that they would admit to being motivated by a rule-idea with the follow-ing content: 'selling drugs is altogether prohibited'.

Theorem (b) would represent an admissible explication of the logic of descriptive legal science and of the first two concep-tions of validity, provided that we are prepared to accept the metaphor of an all-embracing, rational will behind the law. Granted that all that is the law is currently willed by a rational being, a place may be found (as we saw when discussing Bentham's theory) for every one of the logical principles of legal science. In many ways Theorem (b) attunes better with legal— and especially with popular—discourse than does Theorem (d), provided only that we substitute for the personification of 'the sovereign' the personification of 'the law' itself. Information about the content of legal provisions is often conveyed by sen-tences whose nominative subject is 'the law', and whose predi-cates include main verbs which are capable of being understood as verbs of willing or commanding: 'the law requires . . .'; 'the law says that you must . . .' It is possible that, if one could persuade the average citizen to answer a question like: 'Why couldn't there be a law allowing people to sell goods on Sundays at the same time as a law making it a crime to sell goods on Sundays?' he would answer: 'Because it would be illogical if the law wanted contradictory things.'

Against this plausibility of the 'logic of the will' as an explication of validity/1 and validity/2 must be set its dangers for theory and ultimately for practice. If we once admit the metaphor of a personified law with an all-embracing will, we may be in danger of blinding ourselves (as Bentham and Austin did) to its metaphorical character. We may seek to identify the sovereign law-person with some real person or persons, such as legislators. We may try to find a real willer in the case of the creation of each individual legal rule.[1]

More importantly, if theorists merely reiterate the law-will language of every-day discourse, they may commit theory to the will model of rationality as the natural, or even necessary, model for use in unclear cases. If our logical justification for describing legal normative material systematically is conceived as the presupposition of a transcendent will, then we may be tempted to conclude that, if the law is uncertain, this must be because we are not sure what is willed, and to look for some real intention on the point. Now it may well be that will model rationality, in many contexts, has much to commend it as against other models of legal rationality; but we should be clear that theory related to the quite different problem of explaining the logical basis of legal science ought not to pre-empt this issue.

'Acceptability by a rational official' would also represent a possible logical explication of validity/1 and validity/2. If, in conformity with Theorem (g), we accept that legal rules form a system only if they predictably will form part of the motivation of the verbal behaviour of persons carrying out some official role, we can justify denying that contradictory rules are valid/2, since it would not square with the actions of a rational official to accept rules with contradictory contents.[2] We can justify

---

[1] Kelsen attempted to do this. His reason was not, however, the 'logic of the will' which, given his conception of the basic norm, his theory did not require, but his attempt to explain the nature of the legal 'ought'—*supra*, p. 37.

[2] Cf. Dworkin: 'Comments on the Unity of Law Doctrine (a response)', in Keifer & Munitz (eds.): *Ethics and Social Justice*, vol. 4 of *Contemporary Philosophic Thought*, p. 200.

subsumption, for it can be predicted that officials, being motivated by rule-ideas about sources, will only accept individual
rules if they are valid/1 relative to the sources identified by these
rule-ideas. Similar predictions justify derogation; and if the
source-rule ideas effective at any one time are assumed to be
finite, the principle of exclusion is also justified in terms of
Theorem (g).

However, unlike Theorem (b), this approach would bear no
relation to existing discourse; and, as we saw in chapter two, it
raises difficult questions about the practicability of verification,
and has the fatal disadvantage of debarring legal officials themselves from describing the law.[1] Further, as mentioned in the
last chapter, equating system-membership with what officials
do distorts the operation of the value of constitutionality.[2]

I conclude that the sort of rules which are described as
valid/1 or valid/2, and by being so described are made members
of momentary legal systems, must be equated with pure-norm
rules, which together constitute normative fields of meaning.

(B) *Validity within non-momentary systems*

One cannot describe as 'non-contradictory' that 'legal system'
which consists of rules, principles, policies, and maxims, existing
over a period of time as part of the traditoin of one or more
legal communities.[3] Normative phrases which provide officials
with reasons for choosing how to settle disputes may conflict,
and if they do, they are not thereby rendered invalid. Validity/1
and validity/2 do not apply to them.

In an English case involving a dispute between the original
owner of a car and one to whom it had been sold by a thief, it
was said in the Court of Appeal:

In the development of our law, two principles have striven for
mastery. The first is for the protection of property: no-one can give
a better title than he himself possesses. The second is the protection
of commercial transactions: the person who takes in good faith and
for value without notice should get a good title.[4]

Here 'our law' refers to a congeries of sentences and phrases
contained in legal source-materials, which are available for

---

[1] *Supra*, p. 50.   [2] *Supra*, p. 74.   [3] *Supra*, p. 69.
[4] *Bishopsgate Motor Finance Corporation Limited* v. *Transport Brakes, Limited* (1949),
1 K.B. 322, 336 (Denning, L. J.).

settling disputes in cases where legality directs no clear solution (Theorem (k)). Such a system exists over time as part of the tradition of certain legal officials. Its constituent choice-guidance devices—including 'paper rules' in the sense of Theorem (j)—'strive for mastery', in that, where any two point in different directions, sometimes one, sometimes the other, is employed. But they can never be valid/2 or invalid/2, because the fact that they conflict does not mean that only one and not the other can be a member of the system constituted by 'our law'.

Could such a non-momentary system be understood as a mass of rule-ideas (Theorem (f)), or as a complex of rule-situations (Theorem (i))? Given the evidence which is likely to be advanced in support of the contention that such and such a principle is part of a non-momentary system, the answer must be no, for the evidence will not consist of appeals to psychological or behavioural facts. That the principle 'no-one can give a better title than he himself possesses' is part of our law would be proved by pointing to statements in authoritative texts in which that sentence, or other words with equivalent import, have been used.

The constituents of non-momentary systems have in common only the normative function of being able to be used to guide or justify decisions. The meanings they express vary enormously in logical type. Sometimes they enunciate relatively clear goals, like the principle 'the person who takes in good faith and for value without notice should get a good title'. Sometimes they are second-order maxims, used to demarcate the scope of first-order, goal-stipulating rules and principles, such as the canon of construction *expressio unius, exclusio alterious*. Sometimes they are maxims whose meaning, out of context, cannot be specified at all, such as *ubi jus, ibi remedium*. What they collectively express is legal doctrine, the basis of the doctrine model of rationality. But such doctrine is not internally systematized. The system consists merely of the collectivity of verbal formulations. Each member of the system owes its membership, its status as a 'legal' principle, policy etc., to its correspondence with a segment of social reality, that is, with the verbal practices of officials. This correspondence may be direct in that the form of words in question has been repeated (perhaps with trivial variations) in texts treated as officially authoritative; or, in the case of verbal formulations whose normative import is relatively clear even out of context, this correspondence may be indirect in that authoritative texts contain other sentences and phrases with the same normative import. Membership of non-momentary systems is thus an instance of validity/3.

My description of a Theorem (k) system as a traditionary (historic) system does not imply that the choice-guidance devices of which it is constituted are necessarily immune from deliberate change. The United Kingdom parliament could enact: 'As from the passing of this act, the principle of good faith shall be a principle of English contract law'. But if this were all that was done, if there were no enactment of rules imposing duties on officials to take 'good faith' into account when reaching decisions of a certain kind, then there would only be an 'addition to the law' in the sense that it could be predicted that, over a period of time, English judges would be guided to changes in the law by this principle. In other words, the present law—the body of currently valid/2 duty-imposing and duty-excepting legal rules (Theorem (d))—would not have been changed by the enactment. But the Theorem (k) legal system would predictably be different. The reason for this predictable change would be the fact of deference to parliamentary legislation. It would provide adequate empirical grounds for ascribing validity/3 to the newly enacted principle.

Thus, a paper rule, principle, policy, or maxim can only be valid/3 or valid/4. It can only correspond with the (current or predictable) verbal practices of officials, or be (politically or morally) meritorious.

16. VALIDITY, EFFECTIVENESS, AND GOODNESS

Legal science has no need of the third and fourth conceptions of validity when it is exercising its primary function of giving information about the clear law. 'What the law is' is a separate matter from whether the law is efficacious or good.

It is common enough for a lawyer to describe as valid a rule which, whilst it is valid/2 relative to an efficacious system, is not itself observed. It may even be possible to predict of a newly enacted valid/1 and valid/2 rule that it will always remain a 'dead letter', that is, that it lacks validity/3. Kelsen recognized that a norm is valid from the moment of its enactment, before it can become effective;[1] but asserted that it must cease to be valid if it remains permanently inefficacious.[2] This is only true, however, of jurisdictions in which desuetude is a constitutional doctrine. In Common Law jurisdictions, legal rules do not cease to be valid merely through loss of efficacy. This indicates that the principle of annulment through desuetude is not part of the logical apparatus presupposed by legal scientists independently of positive legal regulation.

Nevertheless, the primary function of legal science is not its only proper function. A lawyer would certainly be conveying useful information if he pointed out that a newly enacted legal rule would never be applied in practice. In that particular context, merely to say that the rule was valid/1 and valid/2 would be misleading. But, in denying the validity/3 of the rule, he would not be exercising a function peculiar to legal science. The information about social conditions on which his opinion would be based would be exactly the same sort of information as a sociologist would be concerned to collect if he interested himself in this aspect of legal sociology. It would take the form, for instance: 'that is the sort of statute which the police (or ministry officials) don't bother to enforce; it may be "valid law", but it's a dead letter from the start just the same.' Validity/3 is of great use to the sociology of law.[3]

There is one context in which legal scientists *are* peculiarly concerned with validity/3. This relates to developments in choice-guidance devices. A principle will no longer be valid/3 when it ceases to correspond to an official tradition and so ceases to be part of a non-momentary legal system. If judges in Common Law countries were all to take the paternalist trend, the principle of 'freedom of contract' would cease to be a valid/3 part of the Common Law.

In addition, it would normally be pointless to ascribe validity/1 or validity/2 to rules where the entire momentary system comprising them had no relation to social reality.[4] Hart suggests two exceptions: first, where the object was to describe a set of laws valid in the past; secondly, where the object of

---

[1] *S.L.R.*, p. 1140.   [2] *G.T.*, pp. 119–20; *P.T.L.*, pp. 212–13.   [3] *Supra,* p· 106.
[4] Cf. *G.T.*, p. 437; *P.T.L.*, pp. 46–8, 86–7; *S.L.R.*, p. 1142; *C.L.*, pp. 100–1, 247.

ascribing validity to an ineffective system was to stimulate or strengthen political opposition to a regime.[1]

In the first case, 'validity' is being ascribed to rules in the usual descriptive legal-science senses of validity/1 and validity/2. What is being described is a momentary legal system which was the present law of a community at a particular time in the past, or—where developments in the law are described—a temporal series of such systems. So far as the legal historian purports to describe (rather than to explain) the law at some time in the past, he applies the same logical principles as he would do in describing the present law. The immediate objective is the same in both cases, namely, the exposition of a field of normative meaning; although the ultimate objective is instruction in history, rather than the provision of information which would assist the citizen to predict official behaviour. In principle, the legal scientist who describes the law of the past steps into the shoes of a contemporary legal scientist. He passes no judgment upon the moral worth of that past law.

In the second case, however, where validity/1 and validity/2 are ascribed, as current qualities, to rules forming part of an ineffective system, the avowed political objective means that the legal scientist is departing from the strictly descriptive role. Of course, efficacy is a relative concept. A system will be inefficacious for the purposes of descriptive legal science when there is no significant relation between recorded acts of disobedience and measures of enforcement. Once a system's inefficacy (in this sense) is admitted, it is difficult to see how information about its contents can be 'descriptive' rather than 'prescriptive'. In what sense would a textbook describing Russian Czarist law as it applies in 1977 be informative? Correspondence of a legal system with social reality thus appears to be a pre-condition of descriptive legal science. It marks the boundary between information and evaluation. In this sense, there is a necessary connection between validity/1 and validity/2, on the one hand, and validity/3 on the other.

The same connection does not obtain between validity/1 and 2, and validity/4. For legal science to be informative, it is not required that the law it describes should pass a minimum threshold of goodness. Of course, assertions about legal rules

[1] *C.L.*, p. 101.

may express several validity ascriptions at once. When it is said of a rule that it is binding, what may be meant is both that it is part of the present law and that it is deserving of respect. It may be supposed to be the latter either because the ascriber believes that it is in itself a good rule, or because he believes that there is an (absolute or qualified) duty to obey all the rules of the system in question. Either ground of validity/4 may be combined with validity/1 or validity/2, but theory, in the service of free political discussion, must keep them separate. There must be freedom for the critic to assert that, whilst a rule is certainly part of the present law, it is neither a good rule, nor is it one which there is any duty to obey (even though the critic recognizes such a duty in the case of most rules of the system). For there to be this freedom, the second function which Kelsen attributed to his basic norm[1] must be rejected.

It has been suggested that something like a second, validity-conferring function might be salvaged by virtue of another kind of mixed validity ascription.[2] When a law is said to be valid, what might be meant is both that the law is part of a system, and also that the populus at large—not the ascriber—grant their allegiance to the basic criteria of identification. If such ascriptions occur, they would represent a combination of validity/1 and validity/2 with validity/3; for what would be alleged is that the rule has a long-range correlation with social reality: whether or not it is itself effective, the master rule by which its system-membership is identified has a hold on the popular mind. It is, however, difficult to imagine ascriptions of this kind actually taking place. What adjective or adjectival phrase could stand for: '(the rule) is both law and derived from a master rule which the people accept'? Furthermore, as has been argued, it is implausible to think that there could be any such single master rule, in the sense of a psychological phenomenon (a rule-idea), or a sociological phenomenon (a rule-situation). Kelsen's basic norm, and my basic legal science *fiat*, are neither.[3]

We can, therefore, dissipate the enigmas mentioned at the beginning of this chapter. There is nothing at all odd in legal

---

[1] *Supra*, p. 108.

[2] J. M. Eekelaar: 'Principles of Revolutionary Legality', *O.E.J.*, pp. 25–9.

[3] *Supra*, p. 79.

science attributing 'validity' or legal bindingness to positive legal rules without thereby committing itself to value judgments about the contents of the rules described. Legal science is primarily an informative, and not a spiritually activist, discipline. It takes as its sphere of interest a politically organized community in which coercion is relatively centralized, and takes as its immediate subject-matter the field of normative meaning which, consistently with legality and constitutionality, dictates or authorizes behaviour on the part of officials and citizens. Any normative proposition which forms part of this field of meaning is valid/2. It is in this sense that Kelsen's anarchist professor of law might describe positive laws as 'valid'. He might thereby convey useful information to fellow anarchists, which would warn them of official action which might be taken against them by the detestable regime under which they are compelled to live.

Thus, morality is not of the essence of a momentary legal system. It has been argued, however, that it is so of a non-momentary legal system.[1] It may well be that the rules, principles and policies forming parts of a Theorem (k) system will not continue to correspond with social reality (be valid/3), unless they are thought to deserve allegiance (are considered valid/4). It should be borne in mind, however, that the 'morality' which a paper rule must have in order to continue to be one of the congeries of choice-guidance devices forming part of an official tradition is derived only from the localized ideology of influential groups within the society in question. There is no reason to suppose that all historic legal systems correspond with any principles of critical morality claiming to have universal application.

On the other hand, validity/4 is perhaps the commonest sense of the term 'valid' in non-legal discourse. A valid argument is a good argument and a valid political philosophy is one to which we grant our approval. One who disapproves of the political institutions of a particular society may always deny that its valid/2 laws are valid/4.

It is also true that it is a proper (though not the primary) function of legal science to offer moral or political criticisms of

[1] R. W. M. Dias: 'Temporal Approach Towards a New Natural Law' (1970), 28 C.L.J. 75.

individual valid/2 rules. This will not, however, usually be done by denying validity (validity/4) to criticized rules. What will typically be urged is that a certain legal rule is 'unjust', or 'unworkable'.

17. VALIDITY, EXISTENCE, AND REALITY

The distinctive roles of the first four conceptions of validity listed at the beginning of this chapter enable us to deal with the problem raised in theoretical discussions by the law's amoral bindingness. But theory has also raised a further complication with the so-called 'ontology' of rules or norms, which requires consideration of the fifth conception. It has been urged that a norm, like other things, either exists or it does not; and, since (unlike material objects) its existence cannot be a feature of a material reality, it becomes necessary to assume a transcendent normative reality; valid/5 means being part of such a reality. This problem has seemed more acute, it appears, to theorists whose languages commonly employ the same word to cover the senses of validity here distinguished as valid/1 and valid/3, than to English-speaking theorists, since in English some such expression as 'in force' is most often used for the latter.[1] But aspects of the problem arise in connection with any attempt to unearth a unique and indefeasible quality of existence or validity.

The problem ought never to have arisen. What it means for a thing to exist varies according to whether the thing is an abstract entity, or an empirically observable object or occurrence. Whatever may be true of the latter, in the case of the former we are free to choose the conditions of existence, since the quality of 'being', as applied to an abstract entity, is as much a symbol-in-use as the entity itself. The conditions of existence which we choose may, like the entity itself, be criticized as relatively unhelpful in the cognition of social life, but it would be a mistake to criticize them as not being the true conditions of existence. Their correspondence with reality is an epistemo-logical-functional one only.

Thus, the abstraction represented by a rule-situation 'exists'

---

[1] Cf. *N.A.*, pp. 107–28; Ross: Review of *The Concept of Law*, by H. L. A. Hart (1962), 71 Y.L.J. 1185, 1190.

when the behavioural elements, from which it is abstracted, pass whatever threshold of frequency we care to specify as the conditions for its existence. Hart tells us merely that a rule exists when there is general conformity to a standard, and criticisms, demands, and acknowledgements are common.[1] Such imprecision is perfectly legitimate, because the abstraction constituted by the rule-situation itself is much more useful than would be any exact delimitation of its conditions of existence.

To say that a rule-situation 'exists' is the same as to say that a normative proposition has a certain correspondence with social reality (is valid/3). Such 'existence' is therefore relative. A pure-norm rule may also exist relatively to another rule, where 'existence' means validity/1. But here the conditions of existence are defined: a rule exists (is valid/1) if and only if the normative proposition of which it consists can be subsumed under another normative proposition. Similarly, such a rule may exist relative to an entire system, where 'existence' means validity/2; and here the conditions of existence are given by the four logical principles of legal science. There is, however, outside the context of critical morality, no sense in which a rule can be said to exist without qualification; not, that is, unless we admit as legitimate the fifth conception of validity.

Validity/5 is a metaphysical conception to be found in various forms of idealist legal theory. It is metaphysical in that it indicates a connection between normative propositions and a non-natural, meta-reality, by reference to which they may be adjudged to be 'really' valid.

Kelsen at times appeared to treat of validity in this sense. He said that the word 'valid' designates a norm's 'specific existence';[2] and he referred to law as a 'realm' which 'stands over against reality',[3] or 'juxtaposes itself to reality'.[4] He frequently contrasted the 'reality' which was the object of knowledge of legal science with the 'natural reality' which was the object of knowledge of the natural sciences.[5] Throughout most of his writings, he added to this metaphysical gloss on his theory an analogy with Kant's epistemology.[6] Just as, according to Kant, in knowing nature we assume only one space, so, Kelsen argued,

---

[1] *Supra*, p. 55.   [2] *G.T.*, p. 30; *P.T.L.*, p. 10.   [3] *G.T.*, p. 121.
[4] *P.T.L.*, p. 213.
[5] *W.J.*, p. 269; *P.T.L.*, pp. 19, 86, 104; *E.L.M.P.*, p. 232.   [6] *Supra*, p. 81.

there can only be one normative space which is the object of normative science.[1] If a norm exists in the sense that it actually occupies a segment of a transcendent normative reality (is valid/5) no conflicting norm can be valid at the same time. This explains two of his most puzzling assertions: first, that no one who accepts the validity of both a national and the international legal order can recognize any conflicts between them;[2] secondly, that no one can ascribe validity simultaneously to conflicting rules of law and morality.[3]

I have already indicated that the basis of the principle of non-contradiction is political, not epistemological, so no analogy with Kant was necessary.[4] Legal science assumes non-contradiction between rules forming part of a momentary legal system because legal officials will, consonant with the political values of legality and constitutionality, assume non-contradiction. There is no similar basis for presupposing non-contradiction between international and national law, or between morality and law, for these values would not be violated by an official who announced: 'What I do is required by our law, although it is, alas, contrary to international law (or contrary to morality).'

It is against the conception of validity/5 that the so-called 'realist' writers have reacted. Their reaction has consisted, not in pointing out that the conditions of existence of a rule (as of any other abstract entity) are themselves a functional thought-construct, but in equating the concept *rule* itself with some actual thing or event. They substituted concrete entities for abstract ones. They ought to have been content to point out that rules are part of the furniture of the mind, not part of a transcendent reality. Instead, they sought to show that rules are part of the furniture of the world. Hence, as we saw in chapter two, Theorem (e) equates a positive legal rule with a rule-idea (a psychological event), and Theorem (j) equates it with a paper rule (a concrete set of symbols with a special function).

These attempts to make rules 'real' were not very successful.

---

[1] Cf. J. W. Harris: 'When and Why Does the Grundnorm Change?' (1971), 29 C.L.J. 103, 155–6; H. L. A. Hart: 'Kelsen's Doctrine of the Unity of Law', in Keifer & Munitz (eds.): *Ethics and Social Justice*, Vol. 4 of Contemporary Philosophic Thought, 171, 197–8, n. 32.

[2] *G.T.*, p. 373; *W.J.*, p. 284; *P.T.L.*, p. 332; 'Sovereignty and International Law' (1960), 48 George Town L.J. 627.

[3] *G.T.*, p. 374; *P.T.L.*, p. 329.   [4] *Supra*, p. 81.

A rule-idea is as much an abstraction as is a pure-norm rule. Like other socio-psychological concepts, it is an intellectual construct which may be used to illuminate what cannot be directly described, namely, the complex causal relations between social stimuli and social action. If I say that a rule-idea with a certain content 'exists' as part of the psychological life of a community, I am alleging that a certain combination of words typify soliloquistic assertions which from time to time motivate behaviour. I am not offering (for I could not) a direct description of any psychological events. The rule-idea is an abstraction, and the quantity of effective motivation which is to provide the conditions of its existence is a matter of choice.

The printed characters constituting a paper rule may be thought to have the more usual kind of empirically observable 'existence'. But their reality has very little to do with their function. Paper standards are used to justify developments in the law by virtue of the doctrine which they collectively express. The character of the printer's ink, or the paper on which it is printed—which are all part of the 'reality' of a paper rule—are of no interest in this respect. Furthermore, in many cases there will be no single document which contains the true paper rule; so that, as an entity, it is not a single set of concrete symbols, but rather an abstraction constituted by the visual image which any copy of a certain set of concrete symbols is thought to produce.

The peculiar 'reality' of paper rules—as contrasted with other conceptions of rule—is significant only as part of the causal explanation of legal phenomena. Paper rules are one of the stimuli leading to the creation of the psychological conditions which we may reify as 'rule-ideas'. Any attempt to measure the effect of law, in terms of strict behavioural psychology, would have to begin by isolating paper rules.

Whatever value other conceptions of rule might have as part of a causal explanation of legal phenomena, the pure-norm conception is indispensable to an understanding of the reasoning processes of legal science. Mental constructs do not have a meta-reality which parallels the reality of concrete things; but this is not a sufficient reason for rejecting them. Abstract entities may help us to understand the social life of man and, as integral constituents of certain human institutions, they are part of the social life of man—as law (in the pure-norm sense) is part of all those institutions which practice legal science.

It may also be useful to speak about the 'existence' of such mental constructs in various ways. Validity/1, Validity/2, and Validity/3 are different ways in which it is useful to speak of a law (in the pure-norm sense) as existing. Validity/5 is not a useful description of a law, unless what is intended is a theologically-based metaphysic. In the latter case, a positive legal rule is most appropriately to be understood in the sense of Theorem (a), as the concrete expression of a real (divine) will.

V

Models of Rationality

18. LEGAL DECISIONS

IN CHAPTER three, we investigated the structure underlying the 'present clear law', which is the subject-matter of descriptive legal science. In the humdrum, day-to-day application of the law, there are countless situations in which mere description of this law is all that is required. But, as we saw, there are often topics as to which, owing to the inadequacy or imprecision of legislative source-material, legal science cannot simply offer descriptive information. It must instead formulate generalized or provisional legal rules.[1] Further, as we saw, the statement of positive legal rules may include normative terms and standards whose application to many situations cannot be simply described.[2] In such cases legal science can only suggest what the law may be, or ought to be. It must predict, or advocate, a legal decision.

A 'legal decision' adds a (general or particular) rule to the positive legal rules which pre-existed it. It achieves whatever observable consequences it has through the conceptual medium of the law. If a police officer shoots an offender who is resisting arrest, his action may be legal, but it does not involve a legal decision in this sense, since the action of shooting does not itself add to the law. On the other hand, if a judge passes sentence of death, his act of sentencing does involve a legal decision; it adds to the law, since the subsequent execution of the prisoner is a legal act precisely because it was permitted by the particular legal rule (order) created by the judge.

[1] *Supra*, p. 91.   [2] *Supra*, p. 97.

In the last chapter we discussed various conceptions of validity as they are applied to members of both momentary and non-momentary legal systems. The latter consist of a congeries of choice-guidance/justification devices which may be referred to in support of legal decisions. They provide the foundation of what I shall call the 'doctrine model of rationality'.[1] In this chapter I shall contrast this model with other models of rationality which are employed in developing the law by means of legal decisions.

By a 'model of rationality' is meant a class of reasons which may be cited by an official in order to justify a legal decision when more than one decision can be given without infringing legality or constitutionality. It is not a description of the psychological processes by which officials reach decisions.[2]

Although the models of rationality which I shall discuss are in principle relevant to any official role, they are pre-eminently relevant to the role of 'judge', since it is a feature of the modern conception of judgeship that published reasons should generally be given for any decision. There is a more ancient conception of 'intuitive' judgeship, of a judge who knows what is the just solution for any particular case and need give no reasons. He is King Solomon, sitting under a palm tree and doing what is right by the parties. The judgments of such a judge are not supposed to be bound by pre-existing rules, nor yet to give rise to binding rules which would fetter future just judges. Some adherents of the disputes theory of law have recommended this model of judgeship for modern communities, on the ground that a 'trained intuition' will produce better justice than any decision which purports to be based on legal reasons.[3] Such proposals have never been adequately spelled out and will not be considered here.[4] Nor are we here concerned with the kinds of reasons which are (or ought to be) advanced by judges when they are called on to act, not in their traditional role of awarding binding (rule-creating) judgments, but as mediators recommending a solution to a dispute. The role of

---

[1] *Infra*, p. 143.   [2] Cf. *J.D.*, pp. 25–30.

[3] Cf. H. Oliphant: 'A Return to Stare Decisis' (1928), 14 Am. B. As. J. 71; J. C. Hutcheson jr.: 'The Judgment Intuitive: the Function of the "Hunch" in Judicial Decision' (1929), 14 Cornell L.Q. 274; J. Frank: *Law and the Modern Mind*, 2nd edn., 1949, pp. 118–47.

[4] Cf. *J.D.*, pp. 91–7.

mediator is from time to time assigned to persons holding high judicial office—for example, in the context of industrial disputes —because, as judges, they are expected to be unbiased. When acting as a mediator, a judge must certainly give reasons for his recommended solution, but his recommendation does not create new legal rules and so is not a 'legal decision' in our sense.[1]

There are two reasons for calling the models of rationality discussed here 'legal': first, reflection on the judicial role shows them to be appropriate for developing the law; second, they are peculiarly the business of legal science. If a judge has to make a legal decision which is not unambiguously dictated by a pre-existing binding rule, and his decision will create a rule governing that situation and perhaps also situations of a similar kind, only some kinds of reasons are regarded as available for justifying the decision. It is part of the predictive function of legal science to provide information about available 'legal' reasons, because knowledge of them will add to the predictability of official behaviour, at least of official verbal behaviour. It is also part of its critical function to evaluate such reasons, according to the effect they have had or are likely to have on particular areas of law.

I shall distinguish models most commonly encountered in judicial legal decisions (the will, natural-meaning, doctrine, and utility models of rationality) and consider various theoretical objections to them. I shall then examine one outstanding attempt to subsume all legal reasoning within one coherent theory.

19.   THE WILL MODEL OF RATIONALITY

The chief practical importance of the first theorem deduced in chapter two from the will theory of law (Theorem (a)) turns on its applicability to the interpretation of statutes. If a form of words contained in a document is presented to an official as 'the rule' appropriate for settling a dispute, and the situation is such that the dispute may be settled in different ways without infringing the values of legality or constitutionality, in what circumstances is it desirable to solve the dispute by reference to the conception of 'legislative intent'? To the extent that this is a

---

[1] Cf. M. Barkun: *Law Without Sanctions: Order in Primitive Societies and the World Community*, 1968, pp. 116–49.

desirable procedure, the equation of positive legal rule with words expressing a wish is a useful working concept. For if 'rule' is understood in the sense required by Theorem (a), it clearly makes sense to delineate the area to which the rule applies by reference to what the author of the document intended.

Unfortunately, the question: 'What did the legislature intend?' is highly ambiguous, and would be even in the case of a single legislator.[1] However, many of the things it might mean are irrelevant in the context of judicial reasoning. It might mean: 'What effect on his own career did the legislator intend the enactment to have?' But if it were put to a judge that a minister promulgated a regulation in order to promote his re-election, it would hardly accord with his judicial role to interpret the regulation so as to further this object. It might mean: 'Did the legislator intend to legislate at all?' Such a question might be relevant to the interpretation of judicial legislation. If a judge is faced with a statement contained in a judgment of a superior court (whose decision he is constitutionally bound to follow), there are various reasons which he can give for not applying the rule to the instant case. One reason is that the judge who uttered the words contained in the report did not intend to lay down a rule, or did not intend to lay down that rule. The evidence for this lack of intention may be found in other parts of the same judgment, or in other recorded opinions of the same judge.[2] But the question 'Did the legislature intend to legislate at all?' is not likely to arise in the context of statutes, for constitutions usually specify certain formal acts of voting, signing, promulgation, etc., as the conclusive indicia of statutehood.

The two senses of 'What did the legislature intend?' which are relevant to the interpretation of statutes are: first, 'How did the legislature intend these words to be understood?' and second, 'What did the legislature intend the enactment of the statute to achieve?' Similarly, a written constitution, on one view of constitutionality, may be interpreted in the light either of its authors' understanding of its words or their understanding of its purposes.[3]

[1] Cf. G. C. MacCallum jr.: 'Legislative Intent', *E.L.P.*, p. 237; R. Cross: *Statutory Interpretation*, 1976, pp. 34–40.

[2] Cf. *P.E.L.*, pp. 38, 74–6.

[3] Cf. the authors discussed in *L.C.*, pp. 145–53. Contrast E. H. Levi: *An Introduction to Legal Reasoning*, 1949, pp. 57–102.

When a judge finds, by reference to 'legislative intent', that a doubtful case is included within the scope of a statutory rule, he may mean either that the legislature intended to give to the words of the rule a range of meanings which covers this case, or that the legislature's object in passing the statute would be better advanced if this case was covered by the rule.[1] The rational basis of appeals to legislative intent in both senses has frequently been questioned by theorists on the grounds either that a body of legislators cannot have a single intention, or that it is in practice impossible to discover what were the intentions of the individuals composing a legislature.[2] It was suggested in chapter two that much of what is casually said about the common wills of bodies of persons results from the prevalance of the will metaphysic.[3] I shall assume that the conception of legislative intent, as a rational tool for guiding the settlement of disputes, cannot be defended in terms of such a metaphysic—that it simply is not the case that a legislature has a will which generates meaning quite independently of the wishes of any of its members, and whose workings mysteriously reveal themselves to the trained judicial mind.

A defence of the rationality of will-model reasoning might take the following quite different form: 'When we seek guidance from the intention of the legislature, we mean the intentions shared by the majority who voted for the enactment.'[4] To this it can be answered: 'But the majority may only have intended to *vote*; they may not have applied their minds to the possible range of meanings of the words, and they may not have shared any common view of what the legislation was supposed to achieve.'[5]

In practice, it is not possible to require evidence of unanimity of intention either as to meaning or as to purpose among the majority of a typical modern legislature. What may be and commonly is done, however, is to seek evidence of the intentions

[1] Cf. The Law Commission: *The Inrepretation of Statutes* (1969), Law Com. 21, paras. 54 and 55.

[2] See, e.g., M. Radin: 'Statutory Interpretation' (1929–30), 43 H.L.R. 863; J. Willis: 'Statutory Interpretation in a Nutshell' (1938), 16 Can. B.R. 1; D. J. Payne: 'The Intention of the Legislature in the Interpretation of Statutes' (1956), 9 C.L.P. 96.

[3] *Supra*, p. 30.   [4] Cf. *S.L.R.*, pp. 1138–9.

[5] Cf. Olivecrona: *L.F.* (i), pp. 36–9; E. H. Levi: *An Introduction to Legal Reasoning*, 1949, pp. 27–57.

of certain prime movers in the legislative history of an enactment—although, in the United Kingdom, the reports of parliamentary debates are regarded as inadmissible evidence for this
purpose. If there were clearly accepted conventions for pointing
out who are the legislature's intention-agents, there would be
nothing irrational in looking to the agents' expressed views for
guidance as to the legislature's meaning or purpose.

Supposing that we accept this agency model of legislative
intent—that the intention of the legislature means the intention
of the majority and that the majority delegate their intention to
agents—there still remains a bifurcation between the two
approaches which will-model reasoning makes possible. If it is
debatable whether or not a case is covered by a statute, do we
settle the question by asking whether the agents of the majority
included this case within the range of meanings of the rule, or
do we ask whether including this case would promote the object
they had in view? It may well be that we ought to look at different agents depending on which approach is chosen. It makes
sense to assume that the majority delegate the range-of-
meanings question to draftsmen, since only they are likely to
consider possible ranges of meaning; but that the majority
delegate the object-in-view question to the political promoters
of the bill, who are usually the representatives of the government and their advisers. Different results may well follow,
depending on which approach is taken. For instance, if a statute
imposes a tax on 'vehicles', and some new contraption is invented which may be within its purview, an inquiry into meanings envisaged by the draftsmen might indicate that this case
was not covered (because not foreseen), whereas an inquiry into
the fiscal policy of the government which promoted the statute
might clearly establish that revenue should be leviable in this case.

Judges in the United Kingdom generally eschew any line of
reasoning which makes it appear that they are entering into the
political arena. They therefore prefer the first approach; that is,
when speaking of the legislature's intention, they are much more
likely to have in mind the draftsman's range of meanings than
the objectives of the government. For example, the House of
Lords has held that buildings used for rearing broiler chickens
were not 'agricultural buildings' within the Rating and Valua-
tion (Apportionment) Act, 1928, so as to be exempt from rating.

Whatever the policy of Parliament in 1928 in creating this exemption might have been, the buildings in question could not have been within the range of meanings envisaged as 'agricultural buildings', since broiler chicken buildings were not then in use.[1] On the other hand, one distinguished judge has expressed the view that in the case of 'social legislation', such as the National Insurance (Industrial Injuries) Act, 1946, a 'purposive approach' should be adopted in order 'to ascertain the social ends it was intended to achieve and the practical means by which it was expected to achieve them', rather than a 'meticulous linguistic analysis' of the language of the act.[2]

No general principle, inherent in any widely shared conception of the judicial role, indicates how a choice is to be made between the two approaches. This is a serious objection to will-model reasoning. Furthermore, its practicability is a matter of degree, depending on whether or not there are clear conventions indicating intention-agents and accessible evidence of their intentions. Its appropriateness in some instances cannot, however, be denied. It can be, and regularly is, invoked to exclude 'implausible' interpretations, where legislative history (and consequently the object of a statute) is notorious and where an issue cannot be sensibly framed in terms of the range of meanings of particular words. It is also appropriate where a statute employs legal terms of art, and the courts assume that the draftsman intended them in their technical sense. To the extent that will-model rationality is desirable, Theorem (a) is useful. To the extent that will-model rationality is employed where another model of rationality might be more appropriate, or an unreasoned choice is made between the two approaches to 'legislative intent', Theorem (a) is a snare.

It is essential to bear in mind that will-model reasoning is not being employed every time an official refers to 'legislative intent'. This is only the case where reference is made to evidence of actual intention on the part of agents of the legislature either as to meaning or as to purpose. A judge may often give reasons belonging to one of the other models of rationality and conclude

---

[1] *W. and J. B. Eastwood Limited* v. *Herrod* (1970), 1 All E.R. 774.

[2] *Jones* v. *Secretary of State for Social Services* (1972), 1 All E.R. 145, 181 (Lord Diplock). Cf. W. Friedmann: 'Statute Law and its Interpretation in the Modern State' (1948), 26 Can.B.R. 1277.

that, since a certain decision is justified by such reasons (and is therefore rational), it is legitimate to assume that the legislature intended it. In such a case, despite the courteous nod in the legislature's direction, what has happened is that the will model of rationality has been found inapplicable, and another model adopted instead.

20. THE NATURAL-MEANING MODEL OF RATIONALITY

Where the words of a positive legal rule may or may not cover a situation confronting an official, the matter is sometimes settled with the help of a dictionary. If the words, according to the meaning which they 'naturally' (i.e. according to the dictionary) bear, cover the case, a decision which gives effect to the 'natural' meaning has an attractive appearance of political detachment. The official need not make up his mind on policy matters. He may also give his decision the semblance of will-model reasoning, for he can say that, since the draftsman (the legislature's relevant agent) gave no indication of how the words were to be understood in this case, it must be assumed that he intended them to bear their ordinary (dictionary) meaning. Such cloaking references to an intention which may or may not have been present cannot disguise the fact that the reasoning here employed is essentially distinct from will-model rationality.

Natural-meaning reasoning is very common, in the case of English judges. It is typically to be found in short judgments, in which an arguable point of law is rapidly dispatched. In one case, for example, the master of a tanker, who had discharged sunflower seed oil into the sea, was charged under a statute which made it an offence to discharge 'oil of any description'. The information was dismissed by the magistrates, on the ground that the statute applied only to mineral oil; but an appeal by the prosecution was allowed, on the ground that there was no reason to interpret 'oil' otherwise than in accordance with its natural range of meanings, which included vegetable as well as mineral oil.[1] A court applying will-model reasoning would have looked at evidence of legislative history to see whether the

---

[1] *Cosh* v. *Larsen.* (1971) Lloyds Rep. 557. Cf. Lord Herschell in *Vagliano* v. *Bank of England* (1891), A.C. 107, 144.

intention-agents of the legislature actually did foresee and intend such an application of the statute. A court applying utility-model reasoning would have insisted on the production of evidence to show whether or not discharging vegetable oil has the same deleterious consequences as discharging mineral oil, or whether it has at least sufficiently deleterious consequences to make it desirable to try to deter its discharge by criminal sanctions. To settle the question by reference to the ordinary meaning of the word 'oil' is only a little less arbitrary than to settle it by tossing a coin. This is why natural-meaning reasoning is sometimes stigmatized as lazy and unprincipled, and is one of the sins referred to by such pejoratives as 'formalistic', 'mechanical', or 'legalistic'.[1]

The natural-meaning model of rationality may be defended on two grounds: as being economic, and as tending to maintain the separation of powers. It is economic in that it avoids spending the time of courts and other officials in investigating policy issues. Even in jurisdictions where courts commonly investigate purposes and policies in unclear cases, it is likely that there are many day-to-day applications of legal rules by non-judicial officials in accordance with the natural meaning of words, simply because such applications save time when contrasted with a rational weighing of purposive arguments. Depending upon the importance one attaches to the issues in question, one may term such practices 'a sensible economy of effort' or 'legalistic laziness'.

The natural-meaning model tends to maintain the separation of powers because it enables officials to avoid entering into the sort of policy considerations which legislatures must enter into. However, even if an official refuses to consider issues in the manner of a legislature, there is at least one sense in which he may 'legislate': when he makes a legal decision he issues a ruling by reference to which new (specific) legal evaluations can be made. Furthermore, if his decision operates as a precedent, he changes the content of the general statutory rule for the future. Thus the plea of separation of powers in this context amounts to throwing an onus on the legislature to cover as many details as possible, with the penalty that, in so far as it does not, gaps

---

[1] See the authors cited at p. 136, note 2. Cf. C. K. Allen: *Law in the Making*, 7th edn., 1964, pp. 488–90; Law Commission: op. cit., paras. 8 and 30.

will be filled arbitrarily rather than in the way of creative co-operation. In principle, it is suggested, the natural-meaning model of rationality should not be used in decisions of any social importance.

An argument has been raised that natural-meaning reasoning is associated with the pure-norm conception of rule; that if officials think of rules in the pure-norm sense—as normative propositions divorced from the context of their creation—they will be tempted to fill out the rules in unclear cases by reference to the only available non-purposive criterion of meaning, that is, the standard of ordinary usage of words. If this is true, it points to a serious disadvantage in the pure-norm conception.

This suggestion is, in effect, made by Professor L. L. Fuller,[1] in his response to Hart's article on 'Positivism and the Separation of Law and Morals'.[2] As we saw in chapter two, in his discussion of rule-application in doubtful cases, Hart employs the pure-norm conception of rule.[3] He says that in the area of the 'penumbra', 'men cannot live by deduction alone. And it follows that if legal arguments and legal decisions of penumbral questions are to be rational, their rationality must lie in something other than a logical relation to premises.'[4] Although it is not his object to advocate any particular model of rationality for penumbral cases, he does hint that the natural-meaning model may sometimes be appropriate, when he states that giving a criminal statute the meaning which it would have for the ordinary man may be a socially acceptable policy.[5]

Hart equates positive legal rules with the 'core of settled meaning' of legislative words,[6] that is, with Theorem (c) normative propositions. This, says Fuller, involves a 'pointer theory of meaning', which has the woeful consequence that rules will be applied according to a supposed 'inert datum' of meaning given to the words by ordinary usage.[7] Instead, we should equate legal rules with the expression of a purpose on the part of the rule-creator, and apply the rule, in all cases, in the light of this purpose: 'We must in other words be sufficiently capable of putting ourselves in the position of those who drafted the rule

---

[1] 'Positivism and Fidelity to Law—a Reply to Professor Hart' (1958), 71 H.L.R. 630.
[2] Ibid., p. 593.   [3] *Supra*, p. 62.   [4] Ibid., p. 608.   [5] Ibid., p. 611.
[6] Ibid., pp. 607, 614.   [7] Ibid., pp. 668-9.

to know what they thought "ought to be". It is in the light of this "ought" that we must decide what the rule "is".[1]

We have thus the paradox that Fuller, who is making it his primary business to refute the positivism of authors like Bentham and Austin, nevertheless advocates the conception of rule set out in Theorem (a), that is, a rule as an expression of a wish. He equates a legal system with the 'enterprise of subjecting conduct to the governance of rules'.[2] In other words, he accepts the conception of 'legal system' presented in Theorem (b), save that the uniting will which constitutes the system is centred, not in a state sovereign, but in any person or body of persons who seek to govern conduct by rules. Hence, the rules issued by a club or university constitute, for Fuller, a legal system.[3]

Fuller, throughout his writings, stresses the importance of 'purpose' in our understanding of the law. But he fails to notice the two quite different roles of purpose, which I distinguished in chapter one.[4] On the one hand, unanimity in the rejection of absurd purposive interpretations is needed to make practical deductions possible, even in the clearest cases; but here no evidence of individuals' intentions is required. In penumbral cases, on the other hand, as Hart puts it, 'men cannot live by deduction alone'. Here 'purpose', meaning the proven object of the legislature, may operate positively, as descriptive of one aspect of will-model rationality.

In clear cases, there is no need to conceive of the rule as anything other than a pure-norm rule, as a normative proposition capable of deductive application. It is true, as Fuller says, that the segment of meaning of which the rule consists is not 'innate' in the words expressing it, but derives from shared conceptions of purpose; but that does not entail that we must think of the rule as an expression of some individual's purpose. Nor does there seem to be any good reason to accept the suggestion that, in unclear cases, conceiving of legal rules as pure-norm rules carries with it a bias in favour of the natural-meaning model of rationality. The most that can be said is that conceiving of them as required by Theorem (a), as expressions of wishes, carries

---

[1] Ibid., p. 666.

[2] L. L. Fuller: *The Morality of Law*, 2nd edn., 1969, p. 106.

[3] Op. cit., p. 125. Fuller explicitly rejects a disputes theory of law—op. cit., p. 45.

[4] *Supra*, p. 6.

with it a bias in favour of the will model of rationality. We have seen, however, that this model is not always practicable or desirable. Fuller himself argues that the courts ought deliberately to depart from the known intention of the legislature where it has enacted a statute on the basis of a misunderstanding of a social situation; instead, they should give the statute such an interpretation as would fulfil citizens' expectations.[1] This is to advocate a utility model of rationality, the 'purpose' of the rule being discovered by the judge by reference to the consequences of different interpretations.

The pure-norm conception of rule has the merits and demerits of being neutral as between competing models of rationality applicable in unclear cases. It does, however, clearly indicate the boundaries between clear and unclear cases. In terms of it, the legal scientist knows when men can live by deduction alone, and when they cannot.

21. THE DOCTRINE AND UTILITY MODELS OF RATIONALITY

When a legal official has a choice left to him by the limits of legality and constitutionality, and the will or natural-meaning models of rationality are either inapplicable or undesirable, the sorts of reason which he can give for justifying a decision are divisible as follows: he may appeal either to some segment of legislative source-material formulated in the past, or to the consequences of his decision. I shall distinguish these two approaches as 'the doctrine model of rationality' and 'the utility model of rationality'.

The doctrine model alone is applied whenever, in a doubtful case, a principle, policy, maxim, concept, classification, or definition, is treated as a sufficient justification for a legal decision. The utility model alone is applied when the short- or long-term consequences of such a decision are treated as sufficient justification for it. In practice, reasons of both kinds are often advanced in conjunction. It is typically only with regret that an official will recognize that existing principles point in one direction, while good consequences point in another.

The most extreme form of the doctrine model of rationality,

[1] Op. cit., pp. 130–1.

to be found in the history of both common law and civil law jurisdictions, is what is often called 'conceptualism', or *elegantia juris*. This form of reasoning assumes that the essence of certain concepts given in the historic legal system has a symmetry which must be preserved in the decision of individual cases. For example, in jurisdictions of both kinds it has generally been held that an easement (servitude) must cease to exist once the dominant tenement to which it pertains comes into the same ownership as the servient tenement bound by it. In such decisions, there is usually no question of inquiring into the appropriate circumstances (in terms of policy) for terminating easements; it is of the essence of such a right that it *must* be an attribute rather than a constituent of ownership.[1]

Legal development has often occurred in accordance with doctrines appealing specifically to a legally trained imagination rather than to generalized policy considerations. It is likely, however, that at the present day such pure conceptualism is rare. Commonly, the 'principles' appealed to are authoritative assertions with a very mixed logical status. In part they constitute summaries of leading features of existing rules; in part they embody policy directives for decisions in unclear cases; and in part they mark out conceptual frameworks. This is true of the common law principles of 'privity of contract', or *'respondeat superior'*, and of the civil law principles of 'good faith', or 'abuse of rights'. It is also true of many statements about citizens 'rights' contained in constitutions and other legislative source-materials.[2] As we have seen, the same written phrase may often be interpreted either as a pure-norm rule forming part of the momentary system constituting the present law, or as forming part of the non-momentary legal system of choice-guidance devices applied in developing the law.[3] When the context is the application of the doctrine model of rationality, the second interpretation will be the appropriate one.

The utility model of rationality is employed whenever a judge refers expressly to the consequences of his decision as part of its justification. It is not, however, generally perceived as an integral part of the judicial role to employ such reasoning, as is

---

[1] Cf. M. Rheinstein, introduction to Max Weber: *On Law in Economy and Society*, 1954, pp. li–lii.

[2] *Supra*, p. 114.   [3] *Supra*, p. 66.

the case with doctrine. It is supposed to be for the legislature, not the judge, to decide what legal rules have the best consequences for society, all things considered. Hence courts often clothe the utility model in the dress of one of the other models of rationality.

Where judges are dealing with unclear cases in an area covered by statute law, it is unusual for them to justify decisions solely by balancing good and bad consequences. One would be surprised to find a judge expressly announcing: 'The legislature has not made clear what decision it wanted in a case such as this; I will therefore fill the gap; and in framing a new rule, I will have regard solely to the consequences of such rule.' That English judges are entitled to take this course has been denied in the House of Lords.[1] Such an express acceptance of a political role is thought to offend the separation of powers. In comparing possible interpretations, consequences are often considered, but usually only as a guide to legislative will. It is always open to a judge to say that the legislature cannot have intended a particular view of its meaning to be taken since it cannot have intended to bring about the consequences which would follow.

In an area covered by judge-made law, judges are much more likely expressly to adopt the utility model of rationality, especially the highest appellate courts. The latter, in all common law jurisdictions, are constitutionally free to change any rule of judge-made law, and commonly consider consequences in deciding whether to do so. Further, if common law judges conclude that there is no authority on a point, they will sometimes justify decisions solely by reference to the consequences of their new rulings. Even in the area of judge-made law, however, the doctrine and utility models are more often combined; if a new rule must be created, let it at least have some 'analogy' with existing rules.

Statutory rules may, on their face, indicate that either the doctrine or the utility models of rationality are to be applied to the settlement of unclear cases. As we have seen, such rules may often include doctrinally-loaded terms.[2] Alternatively, they

---

[1] *Magor and St. Mellons Urban District Council* v. *Newport Corporation* (1952), A.C. 189, 191 (Viscount Simonds); *London Transport Executive* v. *Betts* (1959), A.C. 231, 247 (Lord Denning).
[2] *Supra*, p. 97.

may confer on officials express authority to have regard exclusively to consequences. This is so when administrators are authorized to do what is 'fit', or when courts or tribunals are authorized to do what is 'just' or 'equitable' having regard to all the circumstances of the particular case. Often such discretions are not absolute in the sense that any weighting of consequences can be made; but rather the discretion is coupled with directions to take certain kinds of consequences into account and to ignore others.

A common feature of the application of rules which confer discretion on judges, rather than non-judicial officials, is what may be called the 'legalization of discretion'. This means that, although the rule purports to authorize the individual judge to do what he thinks right in all the circumstances, the regular exercise of the discretion (with published reasons and a system of appeal) leads to its encirclement by doctrine. Decisions tend to be justified, not merely by assessment of consequences, but also by the support to be derived from reasons given in earlier cases. The utility and doctrine models become mixed. If there is an established state ideology (embodied in authoritative texts) a judge will be expected to take into account the value-weighting which such ideology gives to the consequences of his decision. On the other hand, if the society provides for competing party ideologies, a judge (unlike some officials) is supposed to ignore the value-weighting which one rather than another of the ideologies would give.

In the development of judge-made law, models other than doctrine and utility are generally inapplicable. Judge-made legal rules are seldom expressed in authoritative verbal formulations emanating from a single judicial pronouncement, but are 'supported' by a line of decisions. If no single judge or set of judges are identifiable as the creators of a legal rule, the will model of rationality cannot be applied because one cannot point to the persons whose intentions are to be discovered; and if the rule is not expressed in a unique form of words, the natural-meaning model is inapplicable since one cannot point to the words whose natural meaning is to be tested. We might call debatable questions about the application of such rules instances of 'pure penumbra'; for, *ex hypothesi*, nothing in the rules themselves—neither their words nor their creators' purposes—point the way to a solution. The competition between the doctrine and utility models of rationality in the area of the pure penumbra has been recognized by theorists familiar with the common law method of judicial decision-making, and sides have been taken.

In *An Introduction to the Principles of Morals and Legislation*, Bentham initially maintained that if reasoning leading to normative decisions was based on anything other than consequences, it could amount to no more than a simple averment of the reasoner's subjective preference—'the principle of sympathy and antipathy'.[1] However, in a note appended upon publication of this work in 1789 he recognized that judge-made law had often employed the (for him) deplorable doctrine model of rationality.

When, in justification of an article of English common law, calling uncles to succeed in certain cases in preference to fathers, Lord Coke produced a sort of ponderosity he had discovered in rights, disqualifying them from ascending in a straight line, it was not that he *loved* uncles particularly, or *hated* fathers, but because the analogy, such as it was, was what his imagination presented him with, instead of a reason, and because, to a judgment unobservant of the standard of utility, or unacquainted with the art of consulting it, where affection is out of the way, imagination is the only guide.

When I know not what ingenious grammarian invented the proposition *delegatus non potest delegare*, to serve as a rule of law, it was not surely that he had any antipathy to delegates of the second order . . . It was, that the incongruity, of giving the same law to objects so contrasted as *active* and *passive* are, was not to be surmounted, and that *atus* chimes, as well as it contrasts, with *are* . . . the goddess of Harmony has exercised more influence, however latent, over the dispensations of Themis, than her most diligent historiographers, or even her most passionate panegyrists, seem to have been aware of . . .

Not that there is any avowed, much less a constant opposition, between the prescriptions of utility and the operations of the common law . . . The Cobwebs spun out of the materials brought together by 'the competition of opposite analogies', can never have ceased being warped by the silent attraction of the rational principle: though it should have been, as the needle is by the magnet, without the privity of conscience.[2]

---

[1] *I.P.M.*, pp. 21, 25.   [2] *I.P.M.*, pp. 22–5.

For Bentham, the mischief of the Common Law was the judicial search for aesthetic harmony between new rules and existing doctrine; the solution was to substitute for judge-made law detailed codifications based on the principle of utility.[1] W. A. Wasserstrom, on the other hand, argues that the development of judge-made law could itself be based on the utility model of rationality. He recommends the adoption by judges of a 'two-level procedure of legal justification'.[2] A legal decision is justifiable if and only if a rule can be formulated which requires the decision and if that rule (consistently applied) could be shown to have best consequences.[3] Such a procedure would be analogous to that type of utilitarian justification variously termed 'restricted' or 'rule' utilitarianism, which recommends that individual actions should be justified by appeal to rules and that rules should be justified by reference to consequences; as contrasted with 'extreme' or 'act' utilitarianism, which requires that each individual action be justified by reference to the consequences of that action.[4]

The doctrine model of rationality, as applied to the development of judge-made law, has recently been espoused by D. H. Hodgson and R. M. Dworkin. Hodgson applauds just that 'harmony' which Bentham found so insidious. It is better, he argues, for judges to create new rules which harmonize with existing common law than for them to attempt to find that rule which will have best consequences: first, it is more efficient, as it avoids time-wasting inquiries about consequences; secondly, it makes judicial decisions easier to predict and thus increases certainty.[5]

The efficiency point grows yearly less convincing, as the body of case law which must be searched for possible sources of doctrine increases; whereas, if it were accepted that the common law should be developed with reference to social consequences rather than analogical harmony, appropriate conventions might emerge whereby courts could take judicial notice of the results of social surveys.

[1] *I.P.M.*, Ch. 16.   [2] *J.D.*, p. 7.   [3] *J.D.*, pp. 138–76.

[4] *J.D.*, pp. 122, 136–7. See generally: S. Toulmin: *The Place of Reason in Ethics*, 1953; P. H. Nowell-Smith: *Ethics*, 1954; J. Rawls: 'Two Concepts of Rules' (1956), 64 Phil Rev. 3; D. B. Lyons: *Forms and Limits of Utilitarianism*, 1965; *C.U.*, pp. 1–37.

[5] *C.U.*, pp. 142–53.

The certainty point is more elusive. Are decisions made by analogy with existing law more predictable than decisions frankly taken on the basis of best consequences? Does the harmony go beyond the sounding surface? Undoubtedly, there have been legal doctrines which made for certainty because of their own internal logic. Much of the common law on future estates and interests in land was developed, in a predictable way, on the basis of the coherent (though entirely metaphysical) doctrine that: 'the law abhors a vacuum in seisin'. The modern mind, however—even the modern legal mind—is unhappy with conceptual deductions from metaphysical premises, however coherent, if they result in rules with undesirable consequences.

There is another side to doctrine. It has always included— often beneath an obscuring conceptual veil—a set of generalized, policy-based maxims. It may be that a utility model of rationality would never entirely dispense with such principles, since they express convenient (if provisional) value-weightings. For instance, the principle of *in pari delicto potior est conditio defendentis*, besides constituting a summary of the effects of certain detailed rules about illegality, also embodies the following value-weighting: 'If the consequences of deciding X are that a person may use the machinery of justice in support of undesirable practices, whereas the consequences of deciding non-X are that a second person will secure an unmerited advantage over the first, the consequences of non-X are to be preferred.'

Superior appellate courts are, however, increasingly unlikely to defer to principles when the utility of a debated rule is seriously in doubt, any more than they are likely to be permanently inhibited from developing the law with a view to consequences by conceptual considerations. It is beyond the scope of this book to investigate the evidence upon which must be based any empirical judgment as to the increased predictability, in various jurisdictions, to be achieved in unclear cases through reliance on principled reasoning rather than consequential reasoning. It seems unlikely, however, that the case for doctrine-model reasoning based on certainty alone would be strong enough to outweigh Bentham's point that, if you are going to give effect to utility in the end, you might as well do so expressly.

Professor Dworkin's arguments against utility-model reasoning do not depend on empirical assumptions about economy and predictability. They are philosophical arguments advanced to support a theory of judicial decision-making which subsumes all models of rationality. Dworkin applauds just that 'ponderosity' in rights which Bentham so scorned. It is to Dworkin's rights thesis that I turn in the next section.

22. PROFESSOR DWORKIN'S RIGHTS THESIS

I have set out four 'models of rationality', each of which stands for a category of reasons which appear as justifications for legal decisions. These four categories (with one qualification) between them cover the ground, so far as judicial decision-making is concerned. If a judge were to support a decision by a reason not assignable to one of these four heads, it would—given the conception of judgeship in modern states—be one which it is not proper for a judge to give. This would be so, for instance, if a judge were to say: 'In making my decision, I am not giving effect to the wording or purpose of any legislation, and I pay no attention to any consequences my decision might have; I advance in its support a principle which is part of the philosophy of a sect to which I belong, and I make no claim that this principle has any connection with the principles of our law.'

The modern conception of judgeship requires a judge to administer 'justice according to law'. What this entails is a duty to apply the clear law in clear cases, and a duty to reach decisions in unclear cases by some combination of the four models of rationality. It is a controversial question whether, in assessing consequences, a judge should rely on his own judgment, or should defer to popular or professional opinion; but 'private' reasons based on merely personal beliefs or preferences are supposed to be excluded.

The qualification mentioned above relates to the possibility of judicial justification of a decision by reference to a principle which is not a private one, and yet is not a member of any historic system encompassed by the tradition of his court; (and so not within the doctrine model of rationality). It may not be clear whether a judge has stepped outside his court's tradition in the search for reasons, for the boundaries of that tradition may be vague. He would have done so, for example, if he cited a passage from Aristotle, for the latter's writings are not legislative source-materials for any court. If the adjective 'legal' is, when applied to principles, to be consistently used in order to demarcate those which are peculiar to a particular judicial tradition from those which are not, then principles conned from such a source are not legal principles; yet they may be considered principles of substantive justice, and so fit for a judge to employ. The judge's conception of substantive justice may direct him to political philosophy, or to popular morality, or to his own intuitive 'common sense' of what justice requires. In such a context, a judge enforces, not 'justice according to law', but simply 'justice'.[1]

Merely to set out the different rationalistic features of legal decision-making is not to present a coherent theory of decision-making. We have seen that the will model of rationality has an inherent ambivalence, depending upon whether the point of reference consists of range of meanings or purposive aims. We have also seen that the doctrine model of rationality entails reference to choice-guidance devices of dissimilar logical types. The utility model of rationality merely indicates consequences as a touchstone, and does not, of itself, spell out how good and bad consequences are to be weighed, nor whether consequences of some kinds ought to be ignored. A coherent theory would set out the resolution of ambiguities within individual models of rationality and, above all, would subsume the different models within a single model, indicating which was to be preferred when they point in different directions. It might also attempt to indicate those occasions on which judges should have recourse to considerations of substantive justice, and in accordance with what theory of justice they should act.

It may be that the modern conception of judgeship is too imprecise to yield a coherent theory of legal decision-making: that there are no accepted canons for choosing between models of rationality, or for choosing between dissonant elements within individual models, so that the practice of legal decision-making is, at some points, irrational. Alternatively, it may be that there are differing conceptions of judgeship in various jurisdictions which yield different coherent theories. In either case, an

[1] For examples in English courts, see J. M. Eekelaar: *O.E.J.*, pp. 35–6.

important aim for jurisprudence is the search for a prescriptive coherent theory. *Ex hypothesi*, this could not be based on a single, generally accepted conception. It would have to be based on a political theory which assigned a particular role to decision-makers.

It is beyond the scope of this book to investigate these questions at any length. I shall examine one recent, challenging attempt to answer them, set out in Professor Dworkin's 'rights thesis'.[1] Although Dworkin has expressed doubts as to whether the law can be said to have a 'function', in the sense of an accepted standard or consistent set of standards for testing the rightness of legislation,[2] he does believe that the rights thesis provides such a function for judicial decision-making. The thesis is of particular relevance to the subject-matter of this book because it suggests that the right answers to questions about judicial decision-making show up the inadequacy of the pure-norm conception of legal system.

(A) *Arguments of principle*

Dworkin argues that decisions in 'hard cases' 'characteristically are and should be generated by principle not policy.'[3] 'Principles are propositions that describe rights; policies are propositions that describe goals.'[4] A right, in contrast to a goal, is an individuated political aim; its specification calls for an 'opportunity or resource or liberty' to be accorded to particular individuals.[5] This is simultaneously a 'descriptive' and 'normative' theory of judicial decision-making.[6] The key to understanding the multifarious elements in judicial reasoning is the recognition that 'judicial decisions enforce existing political rights.'[7] What they do is also what they ought to do. It is true that courts may make mistakes in their search for rights.[8] They may wrongly suppose people to have rights which they do not have, or deny rights which in fact exist. Such mistakes may have the unfortunate effect of changing rights, since the discovery of rights includes the investigation of institutional support, and a mistaken decision may have authority within an institutional

---

[1] *T.R.S.*, pp. 82–90.

[2] R. M. Dworkin: 'Does Law Have a Function? a Comment on the Two-level Theory of Decision' (1965), 74 Y.L.J. 640.

[3] *T.R.S.*, p. 84. [4] *T.R.S.*, p. 90. [5] *T.R.S.*, p. 91. [6] *T.R.S.*, p. 123.

[7] *T.R.S.*, p. 87. [8] *T.R.S.*, pp. 118–23.

hierarchy. This does not mean, however, that the judge has, properly, any personal choice in reaching his decision. There is always only one right answer.[1]

It is suggested that, as a descriptive theory, the rights thesis is either a misdescription or an unilluminating redescription of rationalistic features of judicial decision-making. It would obviously be the latter if all that were needed to establish the thesis were assent to Dworkin's contention that the 'right to win a law-suit is a genuine political right.'[2] It would follow that the thesis is true whatever kind of reasoning is employed in reaching judgment. If a judgment was based on 'policy', that is, supported by reasons focusing on the consequences of the decision for the community as a whole, still the winner would have a right that the decision be so reached. It is clearly not Dworkin's aim to prove his thesis in this simplistic way, for he denies that policy-reasoning of this sort is a characteristic feature of judicial decision-making. If the thesis is true, then the decision follows from propositions about abstract rights, as well as announcing concrete rights.[3]

Dworkin recognizes the importance of the concept of legislative purpose in statutory interpretation. He subsumes it and the range-of-meanings aspect of will-model reasoning under his rights thesis in the following way. The judge must have a political theory which entitles the legislature to take away and confer rights. He therefore must understand the purpose of the legislature as the advancement of some principle or policy through the conferment or deprivation of rights. In this way the judge is able to push the legislative purpose to its proper limit, subject always to an overriding check imposed by the canonical form of the words the legislature chose to employ.[4] Dworkin ignores the natural-meaning model of rationality as such.

His suggestion is obviously not that judges, in interpreting statutes, always articulate their reasons in the language of 'rights'; but that they have at the back of their minds an individualistic theory which holds that all areas touched by legislation are covered by a mass of political 'background' rights.[5] Consequently, whatever they actually say may be interpreted as propositions about rights. The theory is obviously suited to the

---

[1] *T.R.S.*, pp. 123–30.   [2] *T.R.S.*, p. 89   [3] *T.R.S.*, pp. 101–5.
[4] *T.R.S.*, pp. 105–10.   [5] *T.R.S.*, p. 93.

United States, where the statements of rights in the constitution
have turned out to have an extremely pervasive application;
although even in that jurisdiction there may be features of
human action and intercourse—on which legal regulation has
impinged—which are not so conceived. It does, at any rate,
appear to be a matter of controversy whether the Supreme
Court should base its decisions on an exposition of historically-
given rights or on a comparison of social consequences.[1]
Dworkin himself asserts that, in the context of criminal legislation, the rights thesis applies only assymmetrically, because,
although an accused has a right to acquittal if innocent, the
state has no parallel right to conviction if he is guilty.[2] This
may be an accurate reflection of the liberal perceptions pre-
valent in common law jurisdictions.But it surely follows that it
is a contingent question whether there are not other matters
dealt with by law, which are not thought of as subject to political rights at all. To the extent that there are, the rights thesis is
a misdescription of statutory interpretation. Even where areas
of legislative concern coincide with areas conceived of as subject to political rights, the rights thesis does not tell us what
reasoning process is employed in statutory interpretation. For
example, if criminal legislation is described in the light of the
rights thesis, it will be seen as (in appropriate circumstances)
taking away a right to freedom from restraint; but such a description does not indicate whether, in measuring the extent to
which a right has been abrogated, the court will give effect to
natural meaning, look to the draftsman's meaning, or co-
operate with the legislature's over-all goal. That the first alternative is possible may be seen from our example of the sunflower
seed oil tanker.[3]

So far as the doctrine model of rationality is concerned, the
rights thesis again either misdescribes or redescribes in an unilluminating way. We have seen that when decisions are justified
by appeal to some segment of legislative sources, normative
expressions of many different types are invoked. In particular,
I distinguished reasoning by reference to conceptual symmetry

---

[1] Cf. H. Wechsler: 'Towards Neutral Principles of Constitutional Law' (1959–
60), 73 H.L.R. 1; A. Bickel: *The Least Dangerous Branch*, 1962; M. P. Golding:
'Principled Decision-making and the Supreme Court', *E.L.P.*, p. 208; *L.C.*, pp.
133–53.

[2] *T.R.S.*, p. 100.   [3] *Supra*, p. 139.

and reasoning by reference to policy-based maxims. Now these different species of doctrine-model reasoning do commonly employ the language of 'rights', or of right-infused terms such as 'property', 'estate', 'possession', 'capacity', 'contract', 'authority', and so on. But if this is enough to establish the descriptive truth of the rights thesis, then that thesis fails to advert to important differences in reasoning. It is important to know whether, at various stages in the history of different jurisdictions, such phrases as 'privity of contract', *respondeat superior*, or *cujus est solum ejus est usque ad coelum et ad inferos*, were employed because of their intrinsic conceptual appeal or because of the policies they were thought to encapsulate. Merely to point out that they describe 'rights' is uninformative.

The rights thesis, however, may go further. It may suggest that when such phrases appear in the justification of a decision, they indicate that an actual weighing has taken place of the opportunities, resources, or liberties to which, in the court's view, parties are entitled. If so, then the thesis cannot be accepted as an accurate description of all varieties of doctrine-model reasoning. Sometimes, as we have seen, decisions are based upon a supposed need for conceptual symmetry which takes no account of such practical individuation of aims. One of the main contentions of the rights thesis, as a normative thesis, may indeed be that pure conceptualism ought to be abandoned.

As to the utility model, Dworkin denies that it is a characteristic feature of decisions in hard cases that they are justified by reference to their general consequences for the community. He is able to maintain this position thanks to his conception of the 'substitutability' of arguments of principle and of policy.[1] This substitutability is facilitated by his assumption that 'all political rights are universal'.[2] The difference between principles and policies is not intrinsic, but depends on the argumentative force they are supposed to have within the context of any particular political theory. 'The same phrase might describe a right within one theory and a goal within another . . .'[3] Thus, if decisions appear, on their face, to be based on economic policy, one can translate them into assertions about the political

---

[1] *T.R.S.*, p. 96.   [2] *T.R.S.*, p. 94 n.   [3] *T.R.S.*, p. 92.

rights of each and every affected individual member of the community.

If a judge appeals to public safety or the scarcity of some vital resource, for example, as a ground for limiting some abstract right, then his appeal might be understood as an appeal to the competing rights of those whose security will be sacrificed, or whose just share of that resource will be threatened if the abstract right is made concrete.[1]

Dworkin maintains that the argumentative force of a principle is less than that of its equivalent policy: for example, a minority's claim to an anti-discrimination statute might be outweighed by the majority's annoyance and discomfort if the latter were regarded as a policy, but not if it is expressed as a principle.[2] If they are really substitutable, it is difficult to see how this can be so. If 'disturbance to the community' has a certain argumentative strength, how can 'infringement of the right of every member of the community not to be disturbed' have less? It seems, rather, that arguments of principle will have less weight than their equivalent arguments of policy only if they cover a narrower range of individual interests and hence are not substitutable. Dworkin sometimes indicates that this is a necessary feature of such arguments, as when he says that a person's right to protection can compete with another's right to act only 'if that person would be entitled to demand that protection from his government on his own title as an individual without regard to whether a majority of his fellow citizens joined in the demand'.[3]

It is probably true that judges are better fitted to make value choices, the narrower the range of interests involved. But if such a narrowing of range of inquiry is what is meant by a call for arguments of principle rather than arguments of policy, the rights thesis is an arguable prescriptive, but not an accurate descriptive, theory; for, as Dworkin's critics have pointed out, wider-ranging, community-relevant arguments are quite often taken into account by courts.[4] Dworkin indicates that there is very little chance of any critic actually supplying a counter-

[1] *T.R.S.*, p. 100.   [2] *T.R.S.*, p. 96.   [3] *T.R.S.*, p. 194.

[4] K. Greenawalt: 'Policy, Rights, and Judicial Decision' (1977), 11, Ga. L.R. 991, 1003–35. E. Bodenheimer: 'Hart, Dworkin, and the Problem of Judicial Law-Making Discretion', ibid. 1143, 1156–62.

example to the rights thesis, because the substitution programme may be supported by attributing any one of a wide variey of conceptions of rights to the judge who appears to be speaking about policy.[1] The main object of the thesis is not to provide a basis for criticizing judgments but to set at rest fears which some have expressed about controversial political questions being decided by non-elected judges. Hence, when Dworkin and his critics enter the arena, the ringside seat is reserved not for the well-informed lawyer, but for the perturbed democrat. His anxieties will be allayed if he accepts the rights thesis, for he will then appreciate that judges do not make policy, but merely enforce existing rights. It is therefore crucial to the rights thesis, as we shall see, to deny that judges have any choice in hard cases.

(B) *Implications for 'the model of rules'*

Dworkin combines his denial of the utility model of rationality with an attack on 'positivism' in general, and 'the model of rules' in particular. One of the key tenets of positivism, he argues, is that law is exclusively comprised of rules. This leads to the implication that, where rules give no unambiguous guidance, nothing in the law indicates what courts should do. It follows that courts must reach their decisions by the exercise of discretion.[2] Any choices they make cannot be objective, for (says Dworkin) there exists no calculus by which inter-personal comparisons of utility can be made.[3] Consequently, he concludes, what positivists assume that judges do is the infusion in hard cases of their personal political morality.[4]

Dworkin's attack on positivism can be broken down into three stages: first, rules are not enough; second, there is no line between law and morality; third, judges have no 'discretion'.

Dworkin maintains that, in hard cases, there are legal criteria, other than rules, which can be used to justify decisions, and these must be captured by any theory of law. This contention tallies with the argument of this book, that both momentary

[1] *T.R.S.*, pp. 294–327.
[2] *T.R.S.*, pp. 17–22. [3] *T.R.S.*, p. 85.
[4] *T.R.S.*, p. 86. Cf. G. Marshall: 'Positivism, Adjudication ,and Democracy', *L.M.S.*, p. 132.

and non-momentary legal systems are employed in legal science.
If the pure-norm conception of system were the only one presupposed, then justification or criticism of decisions in hard
cases by reference to 'legal' principles would be logically
excluded. Principles of too indefinite a scope to be equated
even with large-scale rules—like 'no wrong without a remedy',
or 'good faith'—could not be called 'legal' at all, unless 'legal'
can indicate membership of some system other than that constituted by 'the present law'.[1] There is, therefore, no need to
seek, as some have done, to fashion a master rule of recognition
complex enough to cover both rules and principles.[2]

Second, Dworkin argues that no positivistic theory could cap-
ture all the legal criteria used in hard cases, because they often
include moral and political elements discoverable by the judge
in the community's values.[3] No line is to be drawn, apparently,
between principles forming part of an institutional tradition,
to which it is the judge's role-duty to have regard, and any
other reasons which he may give in support of his decision.
So long as he can formulate his reasons in terms of rights and
can arrange them within a consistent political theory, anything
goes.

In practice, I suggest, if a reason consists of some moral or
political maxim not comprised within the jurisdiction's appropriate historic system or systems, it will, on that account, be
regarded as extra-legal. The rights thesis involves a political
onslaught on traditional, text-based legal science. Lawyers
should no longer say that such and such a principle is a principle of common law, but not of civil nor of islamic law, because
'*There it is* in our authoritative text but not in theirs.' A tradition
centred on written sources should not be the legal focus.
Instead, if asked whether any principle is a legal one, whatever
its source, lawyers should take up an avowed political stance,
based on liberal individualism. This is a political challenge of
the greatest importance, but not an accurate reflection of existing conceptions of law.

So far as Dworkin's rights thesis has gone, however, it does

---

[1] *Supra*, p. 120.

[2] Cf. G. R. Carrio: *Legal Principles and Legal Positivism*, 1971; R. E. Sartorius:
'Social Policy and Judicial Legislation' (1971), 8 Am. Phil. Q. 151.

[3] *T.R.S.*, pp. 58–68, 338–45.

not make the 'model of rules' superfluous.[1] On the contrary, it presupposes it in two respects. First, the politicization of decisions is supposed to occur only in hard cases, that is, 'when no settled rule dictates a decision either way'.[2] Consequently, the model of rules is needed to distinguish hard cases from others. Second, Dworkin distinguishes the principle relied upon in a decision and the particular rule announced in the name of that principle[3]—a distinction which, presumably, coincides with his distinction between the 'gravitational force' and the 'specific authority' of a precedent.[4] The former consists of a principle which a subsequent judge may reject; the latter of a rule binding within a precedential hierarchy. The model of rules is presupposed in this distinction. It is still necessary, therefore, to explore, as we have done, the logical principles which enable rules to be systematized and the political values which make them binding.

So far as precedents are concerned, I have already indicated that what they enact can usually only be described in 'provisional' or 'generalized' rules.[5] The same precedent may be cited as authority for more than one rule at different levels of generality. The point on the abstraction scale which indicates which formulation binds, and which is merely persuasive (has 'gravitational force') may only be decided in later cases. The more abstract formulations may employ the language of rights, rather than their correlating duties; but there is no necessity for this, unless the individualistic-political considerations underlying the rights thesis have already been accepted.

The third stage of Dworkin's attack on positivism relates to the concept of discretion.[6] If it were true (he says) that judges have a choice in hard cases, at which they arrive on their own assessment of policy, two unacceptable corollaries would have to be conceded: first, that judges have a power which, in a democracy, only an elected legislature ought to have; and second, that they legislate retrospectively.[7] Given the rights thesis, there will be no infringement of the democratic principle

[1] It could be interpreted as meaning that principles take over from rules even in easy cases—cf. J. M. Steiner: 'Judicial Discretion and the Concept of Law' (1976), 35 C.L.J. 135.

[2] *T.R.S.*, p. 83.   [3] *T.R.S.*, p. 88.   [4] *T.R.S.*, pp. 110–23.   [5] *Supra*, p. 91.

[6] 'Judicial Discretion' (1963) 60 J. Phil. 624; *T.R.S.*, pp. 31–9, 68–71.

[7] *T.R.S.*, pp. 84–5.

because, unlike the legislature, judges will not consider general community goals, but only the rights of individuals—something which they are fitted to do; and they will discover the existing position about the winning party's right, and so enforce an existing legal duty of the losing party.[1]

Now contemporary English judges often acknowledge that they 'make law'.[2] But the political significance of such acknowledgements is far from clear, and certainly they do not claim to have anything like the same free hand that parliament has. If Dworkin's contention that they have no personal choice (even in hard cases) is correct, references to 'judicial legislation' *tout court* are highly misleading.

The rejection of both the above corollaries should be set against what may be called 'the intuition of the cynical practitioner'. He may be asked by a client who intends to embark upon a certain enterprise what sorts of conduct he is legally bound to perform or abstain from. He may reply that, in some respects, the position is unclear; but that one can find general statements in reported judgments which have some bearing and, if not outweighed by other considerations, might be invoked by the courts. He may wonder whether the quality of the information would be improved by an insistence that: 'Where there are no clear rules, your duties are uncertain; but, uncertain or not, your duties exist now.'

Dworkin advances a philosophical argument to meet the cynical practitioner and to trump any contention that there are simply insufficient standards in the law to provide unequivocal guidance in every hard case.[3] The argument is a complex one, but I believe that the following restatement of it captures its essence.

---

[1] *T.R.S.*, pp. 85–6.

[2] Lord Radcliffe: *The Path of the Law from 1967*, 1968; Lord Reid: 'The Judge as Law Maker' (1972), 12 J.S.P.T.L. 22; Lord Edmund-Davies: 'Judicial Activism' (1975), 28 C.L.P. 1; Lord Devlin: 'Judges and Lawmakers' (1976), 39 M.L.R. 1. For such acknowledgements in decided cases, see M. D. A. Freeman: 'Standards of Adjudication, Judicial Law-making and Prospective Overruling' (1973), 26 C.L P 166.

[3] Cf. G. C. MacCallum Jr.: 'Dworkin on Judicial Discretion' (1963), 60 J. Phil. 638. K. Greenawalt: 'Discretion in Judicial Decision: the Elusive Quest for the Fetters that Bind Judges' (1975), 75 Col. L. R. 359. J. Umana: 'Dworkin's "Right Thesis"' (1976), 74 Mich. L.R. 1167. S. R. Munzer: 'Right Answers, Pre-existing Rights, and Fairness' (1977), 11 Ga. L.R. 1055.

It can be shown, by analogy to the logic of moral judgments, that there is no judicial choice in hard cases. The careful and consistent moral reasoner may say that the rightness of a certain action is supported by reasons A, B, and C. Perhaps he will be confronted with reasons X, Y, and Z which, he acknowledges, tell against the rightness of the action. In that case, if he remains of the same mind, he will support his view, not simply by averring that 'it seems to me' that A, B, and C on the whole outweigh X, Y, and Z, but rather by giving a reason, A/1. Supposing then he is confronted with a counter-reason, X/1, which, it is alleged, shows that X, Y, and Z outweigh A, B, C, and A/1. If he still maintains that the action is right, he will produce a further reason, A/2, which shows that A, B, C, and A/1 together outweigh X, Y, Z, and X/1; and so on to A/n. At no stage will he say: 'I have a set of reasons for my view, but I acknowledge that, by themselves, they are not enough to support it; to them must be added my own subjective assessment, my "hunch", my (legislative) choice.'[1]

This is a controversial characterization of moral reasoning but let us assume that it is correct. The analogy between the position of the careful moral reasoner and that of the practical decision-maker, including that of the judge, does not hold. In moral reasoning, the pleadings are never closed. The detached moral reasoner may always adjourn judgment. He can say: 'The reasons brought to my attention so far exactly balance, so I will not pronounce on the rightness of the action until I can formulate a reason which tilts the scale; and after that, I will be prepared to consider revising my conclusion in the light of further reasons.' The practical decision-maker is not so fortunate, for he must close pleadings and decide even if he can give no reason, A/n, why the arguments on one side outweigh those on the other. He will be forced to say, having rehearsed the arguments: 'it seems to me that . . .'; 'to my mind it seems clear that . . .'; 'I am persuaded on the whole that . . .' This is all too frequently the position into which judges are forced, whichever mix of the models of rationality they employ.

[1] Dworkin: 'Judicial Discretion' (1963), 60 J.Phil. 624, 636–7; 'Philosophy, Morality and Law: Observations Prompted by Professor Fuller's Novel Claim' (1965), 113 U. Pa. L.R. 668, 686–8. *T.R.S.*, pp. 63–4, 327–30. Dworkin draws a similar analogy between judicial decisions and the conclusions of a literary critic— *L.M.S.*, pp. 71–6.

Dworkin's claim that there is no discretion in hard cases should be distinguished from his claim that, for all practical purposes, there is always one right answer. The former claim is founded on the contention that there is no need to posit judicial choice, because reasons never run out. The second claim is based on the view that, as between the assertion and denial of a legal proposition, there is no middle ground. To deny the truth both of a proposition of law and of its contrary is either epistemo-logically incoherent, or makes implausible assumptions about the truth-ground rules of conventional legal institutions.[1] How-ever, acceptance of this contention is perfectly compatible with an assertion of judicial discretion. One might argue that, given a putative proposition of law (P) and its contrary (not-P), it is always the case that either P is true or that not-P is true, but that the law may sometimes authorize the courts to choose which is true. Conventionally, this is expressed by saying that the law on this point is uncertain, that we need a judicial ruling. In terms of an epistemological framework like that presupposed by Dworkin's argument, we would have to say that each is conditionally true and each conditionally false, the condition being an affirmative or negative choice by a hypothetical judge. Dworkin denies this possibility by referring us to the linguistic practices of lawyers when they employ 'dispositive concepts'. Lawyers speak of a contract being valid or invalid; they never say: 'On the law as it stands, the contract is valid if the court so chooses'.[2] But might not the cynical practitioner say just that?

Such would be the state of the present law. Of course, we can offer reasons, in terms of one or other of the models of rational-ity, why the choice should be made one way or the other; and we may think the reasons are so compelling, and so grounded in historic legal systems, that it would be legally unsound if any but one choice were made. We may give expression to this belief, as lawyers quite commonly do, by affirming the truth of P or not-P categorically. But it is better for legal scientists to resist this temptation, if they are not to mislead. Lawyers should admit that the law is uncertain, unless the contentions in sup-port of a proposition are of the deductive nature which makes acceptance of a contrary view a contravention of legality.[3]

---

[1] *T.R.S.*, ch. 13; 'No Right Answer?', *L.M.S.*, pp. 58, 67–84.
[2] *L.M.S.*, pp. 61–7.   [3] *Supra*, p. 4.

Kelsen is a flagrant perpetrator of the sin of discretionism, which Dworkin attributes to positivism in general. But he commits it whilst denying that there are any 'gaps' in the law. The existing law (he says) can always be applied, since it necessarily includes authorizations to judges to make subjective 'legal-political' choices.[1]

For Kelsen, reasons for decisions, as distinct from valid norms, are not susceptible of 'scientific' inquiry. To such a view, the rights thesis is an admirable corrective. It is the business of the practitioner, and of legal science in general, to tease out reasons which may be advanced in support of legal decisions in hard cases. Acceptance of Dworkin's 'reasons never run out' or 'no middle ground' arguments against judicial legislation might act as a spur in this respect. A proper and much neglected task for jurisprudence is to inquire whether, in any particular jurisdiction, there is an implicit coherent theory which subsumes the four models of rationality under one judging procedure; and another is to assess critical theories about the proper basis for legal decision-making.

A possible competitor, as a critical theory, to Dworkin's rights thesis would be what may be called 'field utilitarianism'. It would differ from Wasserstrom's version of rule utilitarianism,[2] in that it would require a judge, in deciding on the best rule, to take into account the effect on the legal system as a whole of the absorption within it of the new rule (in accordance with subsumption, derogation, and non-contradiction.) Wasserstrom's discussion of legal justification suffers, to some extent, from the typical distortions of disputes theory; for he presupposes 'system' exclusively in the sense of Theorem (k), and 'rule' in the sense of Theorem (j).[3]

The field-utilitarian judge, as a legal scientist, would inform himself of the existing clear law, that is, of a field of normative meaning laying down duties, descending from the general to the particular (Theorem (d)). This marks the area within which he can 'legislate', either by 'developing' the common law or by 'filling gaps' in statutes. He would recognize that by his

---

[1] *G.T.*, pp. 146–9; *P.T.L.*, pp. 245–50. [2] *Supra*, p. 148.
[3] *J.D.*, pp. 12 n., 36–7. Wasserstrom himself recognizes the dangers of these distortions: '. . . it is a mistake to concentrate too much on courts in any analysis of how conflicts are resolved by the legal system' (*J.D.*, p. 9).

decision he creates a new individual rule for the parties, which stipulates a new duty or exception to duty for one or more of them. He may also create an individual rule imposing a duty on an enforcement official. Further, depending on his status in an appellate hierarchy, he may be able to create or recommend a new more general rule or rules which will apply in future hypothetical cases. In deciding, at all these points, what rule or rules to create or recommend, he would assess the consequences (all the consequences he can foresee) of the new momentary legal system which will have come into existence after his decision, or in the case of recommended rules, which would have come into existence if his rules were binding. In addition, he might wish to lend his support to statements of doctrine; but here too, the value of statements would depend on their foreseeable effects in future developments from one momentary legal system to another. He would eschew the natural-meaning model of rationality, and he would defer to will-model reasoning only when the evidence of the legislature's range of meanings or the legislature's purpose was clear.

The relative merits of the rights thesis and of field utilitarianism turn on political judgments which cannot be assessed here. Whether either of them, or some other prescriptive theory, is advanced, the pure-norm conception of legal system cannot be dispensed with. Whatever reasoning is or should be used in hard cases, 'the law' which demarcates hard from other cases, and 'the law' which legal decisions produce, must be understood in terms of this conception.

VI

Conclusion

23. AN OVERALL VIEW OF LAW

THE PRIMARY object of this book has been to elucidate the intellectual processes of legal science. A comparison between different conceptions of positive legal rule and legal system has been a means to this end: first, because different conceptions of 'system' are employed within legal science itself; second, because the differences between legal science and other social appraisals of law can be brought to light if different conceptions of 'rule' and 'system' are contrasted.

In chapter one, I distinguished three senses of 'legal system': (1) as a momentary system of rules constituting 'the present law' of a community; (2) as a congeries of normative expressions of disparate types forming part of the tradition of a body of officials; (3) as an institutional complex centred on courts.

In chapter two, various theorems about legal rules and legal systems were considered. I concluded that the first sense of 'legal system' was to be understood as a normative field of meaning, made up of normative propositions (Theorem (d)); and that the second sense was to be understood as a historic collection of paper choice-guidance devices (Theorem (k)). None of the theorems matched the third sense of legal system; but there were conceptions of rule—rule-ideas and rule-situations (Theorems (e) and (h))—which, together with Theorems (d) and (k), were of assistance in understanding the working of legal institutions, and were also of value for legal anthropology and legal sociology.

In chapter three, we explored the structure of Theorem (d)

legal systems and thereby displayed the logic of descriptive legal science. Structure, it was suggested, is largely a function of that logic, although methodological considerations relating to critical legal science and legal sociology also play a part in determining it.

In chapter four, we considered different conceptions of validity, so as to indicate the different bases on which legal science assigns system-membership in the case of momentary and non-momentary systems, and to disentangle predicates about system-membership from predicates about effectiveness, goodness, existence, and reality.

In chapter five, we discussed models of rationality employed by legal science in 'hard cases'. This involved the most intimate interplay between our first two conceptions of legal system, since Theorem (d) systems were needed to distinguish easy from hard cases and as a snapshot of the state of the law before and after a legal decision; whereas Theorem (k) systems were the basis of one of the most important of the models of rationality, the doctrine model.

Where, in this welter of meta-theoretical comparisons, is 'the law' itself? The answer is that the law is not something one can lay hold of independently of a focus of interest. Is one engaged in descriptive or critical legal science, or in political philosophy, social psychology, sociology, or anthropology? Answer that, and then one can say which conception of 'rule' or 'system' will be the primary point of reference, the 'law', so far as that discipline is concerned. An over-all view of the law must be a phenomenological one which takes account of shifting focuses of interest.

Nor can one pinpoint the law by reference to the ordinary man's conception, for he has no discipline-independent focus of his own. Rather, when he talks of the law, he adopts (more or less casually) one of the focuses of interest which a social scientist (more or less carefully) takes up. He informs another of the law, on occasion, as descriptive legal science informs all the time; or he presupposes descriptive legal information by making judgments about legality. He refers to legal institutions, aiming thereby at the same animal which the descriptive sociologist tries to define. What may be distinctive of the ordinary man's point of view is that he, perhaps more often than the legal scientist, personifies the law—as when he calls it 'an ass'—so that, as we saw in section 15, the notion of a uniting sovereign will (Theorem (b)) is not too far removed from his conception of legal system.

The first two conceptions of legal system are the conceptual reference-points of the practitioner. His training involves a special preoccupation with, and practice in dealing with, legislative source-materials. These two conceptions of legal system represent different approaches to such source-materials. The first differs from the second in that it is exclusively comprised of duty-imposing and duty-accepting rules to which special logical principles apply and which presuppose the official role-values of legality and constitutionality. Only in the first sense of system are rules actually subjected to logical systematization, and only in this sense can 'legal system' yield clear legal duties capable of obedience or disobedience.

If all that legal scientists attempted was to set out the present, clear law on various topics, it would only be necessary to presuppose the conceptions of rule and system indicated by Theorems (c) and (d). When the basic legal science *fiat* is applied to a territorial jurisdiction, the present law (the 'legal system') of that jurisdiction is identified by the sources in the *fiat*'s first blank. In accordance with the principle of exclusion, only constitutional source-rules and rules subsumable under them are parts of the legal system. Conflicts between such rules are to be resolved in accordance with the principles of derogation, by the ranking specified in the *fiat*'s second blank; and, in accordance with the principle of non-contradiction, no other conflicts are to be admitted to exist. How the two blanks are filled depends on the local application of the value of constitutionality. Once the clear law on a topic has been ascertained in this way, the value of legality requires all officials to apply it.

Setting out the clear law on various topics is not, however, the only function of legal science. What I have called 'critical legal science' encompasses the functions of explanation, prediction, and recommendation. In all three contexts, the conception of legal system, in the sense of a collection of written normative expressions identified by a historic tradition (Theorem (k)), may have to be presupposed. The fact that judges share traditions, such as 'the common law' and 'equity', may be a partial basis for predicting rules they will create; and the doctrine expressed by such traditions provides one of the models of rationality by reference to which new legal decisions may be justified.

Furthermore, there are at least two contexts in which mere description of the law is not possible, namely, those in which positive legal rules incorporate cross-references to historic systems, and those in which positive legal rules cannot be unambiguously identified. In the first context, as we saw in section 14, the meaning of concepts contained in the clear law cannot be explained without predicting or recommending particular legal decisions. In the second, as we saw in section 11, there is no clear law at all and the legal scientist must himself construct 'provisional' or 'generalized' rules, justifying the construction by reference to legal models of rationality.

The fact that, in some contexts, descriptive and critical legal science are merged is the ground-rock of objections to positivistic, rule-oriented theories of law. 'How can there be a law which a man may discover without making moral judgments, when very often sensible people (especially judges) disagree about the clear legal solution to a problem?' That they do so disagree cannot be denied. But the point is that 'the clear legal solution' advocated by the parties to such a disagreement is not the clear, deductive solution upon which, as we saw in section 1, the value of legality is founded. In the case of such a disagreement, it seems clear to one man's mind that the models of rationality require the law to be stated in a certain way, but to his antagonist it seems equally clear that they point in a different direction. Where the law is 'clear', in the sense in which it would be contrary to legality not to apply it, there is no need for any of the models of rationality.

Traditionally, academic tuition concentrates very heavily upon instances in which the law is not 'clear' in the latter sense, that is, cases in which practice in applying the four models of rationality can be obtained. A mere recitation of well-defined duties imposed by detailed rules and regulations would be boring and lacking in educational value. Nevertheless, the practical application of legal science requires such information to be given, in the innumerable contexts in which it exists; for information of this sort is of the greatest utility in advising citizens of the ways in which official action could impinge upon their lives.

In recent years there has been a welcome tendency in many centres of legal education to try to broaden legal studies beyond the boundaries which either of the first two senses of 'legal system' might suggest. It is not enough, in many contexts, for a legal scientist to be able to state the present clear law on a topic, nor to be able to predict and join in the application of legal models of rationality to unclear cases. Students of law, so it has been thought, should be concerned with the specifically legal aspects of society, and not merely with the normative field of meaning which can be constructed from legislative source-materials or the paper rules and principles forming part of the tradition of courts. The aspiration has often been expressed as a desire to cross-fertilize the study of law with other social sciences. Some of these efforts have been fruitful, but often puzzling intellectual blockages and misunderstandings seem to have got in the way. It is, with some diffidence, suggested that the distinctions brought to light by the theorems compared in this book could help with some of these blockages and misunderstandings.

There is no sense in which any pair of theorems about 'positive legal rule' and 'legal system' is 'correct', to the exclusion of the rest. They should not be regarded as assertions. They could only be assertions of fact about the usage of words, or stipulative definitions. Actual usage of the words 'rule' and 'system' provides no dominant or central sense of these words; and it would be hopeless to try to effect any change in the existing diversity of verbal practices. What these theorems should be understood to represent are announcements of different points of interest for jurisprudential inquiry. A theorist who indicates his acceptance, say, of Theorems (e) and (f) thereby demonstrates that his concern is with the causal operation of law on the psychological plane. If, without changing his conception of rule or system, he went on to theorize about the consistency or rationality of the overt intellectualizations of lawyers, the discussion would be confused. He would have begun with rule-ideas and, without due warning, moved onto pure-norm rules or paper rules. Anthropologists and sociologists, on the one hand, and lawyers, on the other hand, are often at cross-purposes when they seek to combine or compare their knowledge about particular cultures; for while the former speak, generally, of rule-situations, the latter speak, generally, of pure-norm rules.

What is it, after all, that is specifically 'legal' about a society, apart from our first two conceptions of legal system—that is, apart from the present law, and written doctrine? The answer is, I suggest, as follows.

So far as 'rules' are concerned, there are legal rule-ideas from time to time introduced into the popular consciousness by the promulgation and enforcement of pure-norm rules. How widespread this process is, how effective, and whether it is practical with some kinds of rules but not with others, are questions needing empirical research, but to which speculations of a political-theoretical kind may give provisional answers. It seems likely that they are of the greatest importance in the education of legal officials (especially judges)—that is, constitutional source-rule-ideas are an important part of the motivating ideology of such officials. There are also legal rule-situations, which are the 'living law' that sociologically-minded lawyers are anxious to investigate. They are the only observable 'law' in small, non-literate, tribal societies, and in developed societies they can be contrasted with law in the books (the pure-norm law). The comparison between pure-norm legal rules and legal rule-situations is the best contribution which legal scientists, *qua* legal scientists, can make to the sociology of law.

So far as 'legal system' is concerned, there is the third sense distinguished here, namely, an institutional complex centred on courts. This is something which a legal scientist is not by training well equipped to investigate; but neither is a sociologist without a legal education, for the central officials in the system have, as part of their roles, the logical principles and values of legal science. Here, above all, cross-fertilization is called for. Everyday legal-science, and much of rule-based legal theory, takes legal institutions, like courts, for granted. Yet there are contexts in which stating the law—describing the legal system in the first sense—cannot be done without reference to features of these institutions which are not rule-governed. Two such contexts have been referred to in this book: in section 9, we saw that, where there is uncertainty as to constitutional source-rules (for example, in relation to British entry into the European

Economic Community), describing the law is something that cannot be satisfactorily attempted without speculation about the political beliefs and attitudes of judges and other officials; and, in section 11, we saw that authority is accorded to 'wrong' judicial decisions, not because of any rule allowing them to make any decisions they like, but because of widespread institutional deference. The actual significance of these beliefs and attitudes and the practical limits of this deference are features of the 'legal system' in the third sense.

An adequate legal sociology cannot make do with Theorems (c), (d), (j), and (k), but neither can it dispense with them. Dissatisfaction with the detachment of traditional legal studies should not induce us to throw out the baby with the bath water —to try to pretend that 'real' law is not what is written in books, but rather some specialized social structure or social force. Whatever our particular focus of interest, lawyers in modern, interventionist states are going to go on describing as 'law' the reconstructed contents of legislative source-materials. The thing to do, if our aim is 'social relevance', is to recognize that law, as the subject-matter of traditional legal science, is a series of fields of normative meaning and of historic collections of written doctrine, and to move out into society to discover its practical effects.

To achieve an overall view of the law of a modern state, none of the three conceptions of legal system can be taken in isolation, for each one takes the other two as given. The law is a kaleidoscope consisting of these three enmeshed conceptions of system. The observer shapes it into the pattern he wants to see.

Index